World University Library

The World University Library is an international series
of books, each of which has been specially commissioned.
The authors are leading scientists and scholars from all over
the world who, in an age of increasing specialisation, see the
need for a broad, up-to-date presentation of their subject.
The aim is to provide authoritative introductory books for
university students which will be of interest also to the general
reader. The series is published in Britain, France, Germany,
Holland, Italy, Spain, Sweden and the United States.

David Caute

The Left in Europe

since 1789

World University Library

McGraw-Hill Book Company
New York Toronto

Library of Congress Catalog Card Number: 64–66177
Filmset by BAS Printers Limited, Wallop, Hampshire, England
Printed by
Officine Grafiche Arnoldo Mondadori, Verona, Italy

Contents

List of abbreviations

CFTC	Confédération française des Travailleurs Chrétiens
CGIL	Confederazione generale italiana del Lavoro
CGL	Confederazione generale del Lavoro
CGT	Confédération générale du Travail
CGTU	Confédération générale du Travail unitaire
CNT	Confederación Nacional de Trabajo
FAI	Federación Anarquista Ibérica
IWMA	International Working Men's Association
KPD	Kommunistische Partei Deutschlands
LO	Swedish Workers' Confederation
POUM	Partido Obrero de Unificación
PSI	Partito socialista italiano
RDR	Rassemblement Démocratique Révolutionnaire
RPF	Rassemblement du Peuple Français
SDF	Social Democratic Federation
SPD	Sozialdemokratische Partei Deutschlands
SR's	Socialist Revolutionaries
UGT	Unión General de Trabajadores
USPD	Unabängige Sozialdemokratische Partei Deutschlands

PART ONE

What is the Left ?

Symbol of the modern Left at the
moment of its birth – the revolutionary
'sans-culotte'. This romanticised
representation, taken from a
Savoyard festival of 1792, lacks, perhaps,
the authentic lean and hungry look.

1 Fallacies and confusions

The terms 'Left' and 'Right' have become an essential part of the language of politics and history at both the popular and sophisticated levels. A product of the French revolution and of the widespread European procedure whereby the 'radicals' sit on the left side of the legislative chamber, as viewed from the president's chair, and the conservatives on the right side, this polarisation has for some time past suggested the most fundamental cleavage in modern society, a conflict of principle, attitude and policy.

Yet the Left is as frequently invoked as it is rarely defined. And when it is defined it is usually defined wrongly, without historical perspective. Left and Right, like Jacob and Esau, have always been fomentors of passion and resentment, of prejudice and adulation. The Left, it must be admitted, had a bad start; the New Testament no less than the Old treats the Right as symbolising the good and the Left the bad. 'And he shall set the sheep on his right hand, but the goats on his left' (Matthew 25. 33). Again: 'I say unto you, Hereafter shall ye see the Son of man sitting on the right hand of power . . . ' (Matthew 26. 64 and Mark 14. 62).

But a modern world of freemasons, radicals and socialists have made a virtue out of necessity and turned the tables; in recent times the Left has acquired a distinctly favourable emotional connotation, suggesting progress and enlightenment. A survey conducted recently by the *Institut Français d'Opinion Publique* in Paris revealed that the supporters of a marginal party tend more readily to call it a party of the Left than do its opponents. Thus while the general public regarded the MRP as being of the Right, its own adherents did not. Politicians have long since recognised the implications of this general attitude and they have, perhaps not without a touch of cynicism, shared it. The moderately conservative Democratic Alliance formed in France in 1901 and led by Poincaré and Tardieu was represented in the Chamber of Deputies by groups calling themselves variously Left Republicans, the Democratic Left and Left Independants. Nor has this trend applied to France alone. More recently a liberal writer in Britain claimed that 'by any strict use of language Liberals are the true Left, the real progressives.'[1]

Thus more people than perhaps realise it, scholars included, will be offended by any definition of the Left which seems to exclude them.

One of the most common and dangerous tendencies among writers is to employ the term 'the Left' empirically in different senses on different occasions, on the assumption that each usage is intuitively justified. Inevitably contradictions appear and result in illogicality. Three statements discussing English politics in the 1930's may be quoted here as examples of such confusion.

1 In 1935 it was 'international political events that now sent people to the Left'.

2 'The Labour Party had long since ceased to be Left, and Left activities were without the sanction of Labour Party officials.'

3 'At the same time, popular fronts of all the Left groups were being formed in France and Spain, and the extreme Left wanted a similar front in Britain.'[2]

A revolutionary committee room during the reign
of terror which climaxed the left-wing phase of the
French revolution, in 1793–4. The Jacobins were entitled
to meet force with force and to take energetic measures
against reactionary agitation in the departments.
But by 1793 the revolution had begun to consume its own children.

At first sight each statement seems reasonable enough, but reflection on the actual history of the period brings out the incon-
sistencies. If the Labour Party had 'ceased to be Left,' and if it was
'international political events' which now sent people to the Left,
how was it that the Fulham by-election of 1935, which is universally
acknowledged to have reflected adversely on the government's
foreign policy, resulted in a dramatic success for the Labour Party?
And if the *Front populaire* in France and the *Frente popular* in Spain
consisted of 'all the Left groups,' does this mean that the French
Radicals and the Azãna liberals were on the Left while the Labour
Party was not? All the evidence points against this. Finally, how
could the 'extreme Left' in England want a popular front 'of all the
Left groups' if the Labour Party had long since ceased to be of the
Left? In fact, statements 1 and 3 are entirely accurate and it is only
the error in statement 2 which makes the three statements, when
taken in conjunction, absurd.

Some fallacies examined

There is every value in establishing the limits of a fundamental concept which one is compelled to employ frequently. When and where
the Left has existed, what historical factors have contributed to its
growth or decline, from what social classes it has tended to draw
support – these are questions which can be answered only after a
viable model of the Left has been constructed. One cannot, of
course, *prove* that the term fits one model and no other because
words are inherently democratic and incapable of complete expropriation. A further difficulty arises from the fact that the method of
argument, or model-building, must necessarily rest on the assumption that certain movements, men or policies are almost unanimously acknowledged to be of the Left and others to be of the
Right, or non-Left. If, for example, I am told that social reformers
per se are of the Left, and I reply 'but what of Bismarck and the
Shah of Persia?', then my objection, to be effective, depends on
mutual agreement that Bismarck and the Shah are not in fact men

of the Left. Conceptually, the investigation passes from clearly defined territory to the disputed borderlands, from the familiar to the obscure. But this conceptual, or horizontal passage can be given added substance by an historical, or vertical inquiry tracing a developing European political tradition.

Before advancing a positive definition of the Left, it will be useful to examine some of the widely held fallacies and confusions which have accumulated around this question. To many people, the Left vaguely suggests an attitude towards the *condition humaine* – an attitude embracing optimism, a faith in science and rationality, love of liberty, egalitarianism, sympathy for the oppressed, anti-racism, pacifism, anti-clericalism, hostility to authority, and so forth. There can be no doubt at all that the Left has frequently exhibited these and similar qualities; the issue, however, is whether such qualities and attitudes, viewed either separately or in conjunction, provide a satisfactorily *exclusive* definition of the Left. In practice, they fail to do so, simply because it can be shown that they cannot be invariably associated with the Left; or that they may equally be associated with the Right; or that they are too ephemeral to provide a sound basis of definition. It will suffice here to examine a few of the more obvious attitudes and qualities.

Optimism: The Left, apparently, is essentially optimistic about man and his future. Professor Talmon writes that 'the Left proclaims the essential goodness and perfectibility of human nature. The Right declares man to be weak and corrupt.'[3] According to George Orwell, the Left inherited the belief that truth will prevail and that man is naturally good but corrupted by his environment. Such points of view have certainly been widespread on the Left, particularly among anarchists, but one notices that Georges Sorel and a number of revolutionary syndicalist leaders on the one hand, and the French crypto-Marxist existentialists on the other deliberately extracted from the Marxist dialectic its built-in, determinist optimism about the future of man and society. 'No utopias!' was the slogan. A better society was regarded as something to be striven for by an act of will based on an ethical choice, and not as a consequence of any certainty about the perfectibility of man. How many men of the Left would today view as anything but utopian Herbert Read's assurance that the abolition of poverty and inequality would lead to the total extermination of crime?

Rationalism, intelligence: 'The intellectual, the man of theory,' Mr E. H. Carr has written, 'will gravitate towards the Left just as naturally as the bureaucrat, the man of practice, will gravitate towards the Right.'[4] While the radical philosopher Alain claimed that '*est de gauche . . . le héros d'intelligence*', Dionys Mascolo asserts that the artist's vocation is inherently *de gauche;* there can be no great work of the Right.[5] This sort of opinion is the more commonly held firstly because the Left has developed an exaggerated notion of its own calibre, and secondly because the intellectual foundations of the Left can in part be traced to eighteenth century rationalism, to the enlightenment. But 'reason,' theory and art do not belong exclusively to the Left. Among the French writers, one need only recall Chateaubriand, Barrès, Claudel, even Maurras; among the Russians, Dostoyevsky; among the Spanish, Unamuno. Burke was surely a man of theory even in his distrust of theories. Hegel revered the Prussian monarchy.

Liberty: Love of liberty is too ambiguous a formula to provide a water-tight definition of the Left. The *Institut Français d'Opinion Publique* discovered that Parisians of the Left, when presented with a list of values, made liberty their top priority; but so also did Parisians of the Right. The word suggested a different state of affairs for the two groups. A liberal writes that the true criterion of leftism must be concern for individual opportunity, adding that by this criterion many so-called leftist parties standing for state control and regulation are in fact among the most reactionary. 'I want freedom to conduct my own business in my own way but you, my employee, desiring freedom from the fear of poverty or unemployment, seek to bind me with regulations.' The coin of free-

14

Launched by Gracchus Babeuf in 1794,
this journal provided an organ
for the ideas which later appeared in
the *Manifesto of the Equals* (1796).
Following the abortive communist *coup* of
that year, Babeuf and his colleagues were executed.

dom has its positive and negative faces. If it is the case that the Left
has one concept of freedom and the Right another, then this only
confirms that the Left cannot be distinguished by its love of liberty.

Equality: This is a theme which cannot be so easily dismissed,
and we shall have occasion to return to it later. Undoubtedly the
Left has displayed a stronger egalitarian tendency than has the
Right. But can we always distinguish the Left by its attachment to
'equality'? If so, to what type of equality, and in what degree? 'To
the Left,' we are told, 'men are by nature endowed with an ultimate
equality of natural virtue; to the Right they are not.'[6] This would
certainly be true of the communist Gracchus Babeuf who, in the
Manifesto of the Equals (1796), declared; 'We are all equal are we
not? . . . Let there be no difference between human beings but in
age and sex! Since all have the same needs and faculties, let there be
for all one education and one standard of life.' But few men of the
Left have subsequently assumed so extreme a position. Louis
Blanc, in pleading for equality of wages in 1848, argued that,
'superior intelligence gives no more claim than superior physical
force: it only creates a duty.' If Blanc agrees with Babeuf that men
have the same needs, he has parted company with him on the
question of faculties. In 1875 Marx criticised the Gotha Programme
of the German socialists for speaking of equal rights; men, he
said, were not equal in their productive capacity. The belief in the
role of 'conscious minorities' prevalent among certain anarchists
and revolutionary syndicalists implied a strong presupposition of
human inequality. The syndicalist Hubert Lagardelle wrote that
parliamentary democracy 'starts from a necessary fiction; that all
men . . . have the same worth, sharing the same rights . . . "Workers'
democracy" relies essentially on the organised groups of the proletariat . . . The conception of an abstract equality gives way here
to the notion of a real differentiation.'

The Left, then, has not been agreed about men's abilities, faculties or 'natural virtue.' Nor, indeed, has there been unanimity on
the subject of human needs and rewards. Babeuf, Blanc, and the

LE TRIBUN DU PEUPLE, (1)

O U

LE DÉFENSEUR

DES DROITS DE L'HOMME;

EN CONTINUATION

DU JOURNAL DE LA LIBERTÉ DE LA PRESSE.

Par Gracchus BABEUF.

Le but de la société est le bonheur commun. *Droits de l'Homme*, art. Ier.

Du 14 *Vendémiaire*, l'an 3me. de la République.

Pas rapides et imposans que fait le peuple pour recouvrer ses droits et completter la révolution du 9 thermidor.

Noms de toutes les sections qui ont adhéré à la mémorable pétition de la société ci devant électorale, qui demanda l'anéantissement de toute tyrannie, les droits, la liberté et le bonheur du peuple.

Preuves sérieuses de l'existence d'une faction des défenseurs des droits de l'Homme, et combien elle se grossit.

Les journées des 10 et 11 vendémiaire seront mar-

---

(1) Je change de titre ainsi que j'ai annoncé que je le

A detail from a painting of Pierre-Joseph Proudhon by Gustave Courbet. The intellectual father of the modern anarchist movement, Proudhon was opposed equally to socialism and to capitalism. He advocated instead a 'mutualist' or co-operative society, without government. Popular among the French artisan class, he was imprisoned after the revolution of 1848 for his journalistic agitation. The painter Courbet was later a leader of the Paris Commune of 1871.

anarchist Kropotkin desired the implementation of the 'to each according to his needs' formula immediately, and Marx ultimately, but others have taken a more cautious view. Proudhon and Bakunin wanted to know who would judge needs. Raymond Aron severely qualifies the left-wing quest for equality as being 'against the privileges of birth and wealth,' while the *Institut Français d'Opinion Publique* recorded that although some men on the Left envisaged a total suppression of 'inequality,' others expected only a partial suppression to prove feasible. In fact, the simple statement that all men are equal finally resolves itself into the truism that they are all members of the human race. There we may leave the subject of equality for the time being.

The Left is sometimes regarded as being distinguished by *sympathy for the suffering and exploited*. According to one view, 'of the emotions, only two can drive men into politics: love of power, or the capacity for outrage. One drives them to the Right, the other to the Left.'[7] J.-M. Domenach, reflecting on the United States, asks, 'can one speak of a Left in a country where the simple feeling of human solidarity with the suffering and oppressed has become blunted?'[8] Claude Lanzmann maintains that 'the Left . . . is defined very precisely by its will to abolish the exploitation of man by man.'[9] But in practice love of power and a sense of social outrage combine and fuse to make a Robespierre, a Lenin, even an Ernest Bevin. It is quite true that the Left has shown sympathy for the suffering and oppressed, but the question is – has the Left alone done so? Shaftesbury, Oastler and Sadler, all Tories, were outraged hardly less than Engels by the condition of the English working class at the period of rapid industrialisation. Exceptional sympathy for the suffering can appear in a Nightingale or a Schweitzer without translating itself into any specific political bias. Finally, if the Left endeavours to abolish 'exploitation,' as it does, such a word can be usefully descriptive of a particular activity or situation only in a subjective sense. As with liberty, so with exploitation; your 'exploitation' is my 'free enterprise;' I say that you exploit your slaves while you maintain that they would be lost without you.

In this context it must be recalled that social reformers and states-men whose legislation is aimed at the relief of poverty are not in-variably of the Left. Bismarck pioneered an embryonic welfare state at the very moment of outlawing the Socialist Party. Disraeli was more active than Gladstone in domestic welfare schemes. The United States Steel Corporation attempted to break the power of unionism at the turn of the century by introducing its own social services, insurance and pension schemes.

The Left is frequently regarded as standing for a number of 'en-lightened' attitudes on contentious social and racial issues, of which two of the more prominent will be examined briefly.

Anti-racism: The *Institut Français d'Opinion Publique* concluded that the Right in Paris is generally more anti-semitic and racist than the Left. On the other hand, when in July 1959 a British Gallup poll investigated public opinion about the power of Jews in general, of the Labour supporters questioned thirty-eight per cent answered that Jews had more power than was their due, while only thirty per cent of the Conservative supporters and twenty-seven per cent of the Liberals were of the same opinion. The French Communist Party suffered a wave of anti-semitism in 1948 after Jules Moch, the Jewish Socialist Minister of the Interior, had resorted to tough measures against strikers. At the time of the Algerian war, the Party leaders admitted that many of their followers were prejudiced against the Moslems, including those living in France.

Anti-war, pacifism: The Left, it is often said, is opposed to war, which the Right is inclined to regard as being periodically inevit-able. But history does not confirm this generalisation. In the early nineteenth century, it was normally the Right, the dynasties, which feared war and the social forces liable to be unleashed by aggressive patriotism. The communist Barbès, during his brief hour in posses-sion of the Hôtel de Ville in May 1848, issued a decree threatening war against Germany and Russia unless they forthwith restored Polish sovereignty. Marx had no objection to a war of liberation

directed against Tsarist Russia. Carnot's army of 1793 – and Zhukov's of 1944 – continue to be widely revered on the Left.

Yet another common misconception concerns the Left's supposedly hostile reaction to the church, to religion, to government, indeed to authority in general. Here again we find that what may be true of one country and one period of time is less true of other countries and other generations.

Anti-religion, anti-clericalism: Acute as was the conflict before, during and after the French revolution between the forces of rationalism, materialism and revolt on the one hand and those of religion, faith and order on the other, it was after all Robespierre who exalted the cult of the Supreme Being. For him, as for the communist revolutionary Buonarroti, atheism was synonymous with immorality and cynicism. In Britain, the labour movement developed close links with religious nonconformism. When questioned in 1929, only eight out of 249 Labour MP's declared themselves to be agnostics or atheists. Whereas in France the Catholics within any social class are less inclined to support the Left than the non-Catholics, in modern Britain, according to one source, fifty-one per cent of the Catholics vote Labour and only thirty-three per cent Conservative. Anti-clericalism has always been strong within the French, Italian and Spanish Lefts, but post-war France has experienced a proliferation of socialist, and often neo-Marxist movements having a Christian basis. In any case the French Right, as René Rémond points out, has by no means adopted a uniformly pro-clerical stance.

Anti-authority, anti-government: The anarchists, syndicalists and Marxists have all looked forward to the eventual disappearance or 'withering away' of the state, to the replacement of the 'government of people' by the 'administration of things.' Elsewhere, however, such a prognostication has been regarded as impossibly utopian. That the Left has more often than not opposed the powers-that-be is simply due to the fact that these powers have more often than not represented the Right or Centre. Can we afford to exclude from the Left all those who wished to transform governments, and their social basis, rather than to abolish them – the Jacobins, the Chartists, Louis Blanc, Lassalle, Mazzini, Garibaldi, the Labour Party and the reformist socialists in general, indeed the greater part of the European socialist movement in this century?

There is an extreme view that the Left automatically ceases to be such on assuming power. According to George Orwell, 'the whole left-wing ideology . . . was evolved by people who had no prospect of attaining power.'[10] But the self-consciousness of the Jacobins about the possible misuses of power and Trotsky's insistence that the revolution must become permanent if it were not to ossify are two of many examples which suggest a different conclusion. No one would claim that the Paris Commune or Blum's Popular Front government had, by the time of their fall, ceased to be left-wing. Mr E. H. Carr has observed that the Left in office is inclined to move to the right while retaining its left labels. This is the type of question which needs to be examined in a historical perspective, but free from the unjustifiable assumption that the Left and power are mutually contradictory.

The sociological fallacy

It should be clear then that many of the attitudes, social opinions, emotional reflexes and broad ideals which are loosely associated with left-wing movements cannot in themselves, taken either separately or in conjunction, be regarded as providing a dispassionate and objective definition of the Left. However, two further hypotheses of a quite different order, advanced by reputable historians and sociologists, demand some attention.

'The right,' writes Robert M. MacIver, 'is always the party sector associated with the interests of the upper or dominant classes, the left the sector expressive of the lower economic or social classes, and the centre that of the middle classes.'[11] W. G. Runciman adds that 'the sociological distinction between Left and Right . . . basically it is nothing other than the perennial argument between the poor and the rich.'[12]

It is on the basis of this approach that S. M. Lipset has defined the Peronist movement in the Argentine which drew support from the workers and landless peasants and was opposed generally by the landlords and industrialists, yet was nationalistic, militaristic, élitist, in many ways fascist. Professor Lipset comments: 'If Peronism is considered as a variant of fascism, then it is a fascism of the left because it is based on the social strata who would otherwise turn to socialism or communism as an outlet for their frustrations.'[13] Mr Runciman agrees and comments, 'in a sense, therefore, Peronism could be labelled a Rightism of the Left,' as compared with the Salazar régime in Portugal, a Rightism of the Right (i.e. based on the upper classes).[14] He goes on to draw the conclusion that 'the ideological and sociological senses of Left and Right will very often coincide, but they need not necessarily do so.'

Unfortunately, Lipset and Runciman, and probably MacIver, are victims of a single confusion, a confusion which, if not dispelled, is liable to frustrate a clear understanding of the nature of the Left in Europe or elsewhere. In 1951 more French workers voted for de Gaulle's *Rassemblement du Peuple Français* (RPF) than for the Socialist Party. Does this – to return to MacIver's argument – mean that the RPF was more 'expressive' of the workers than was the Socialist Party, simply because it obtained a larger share of their vote? If so, it would necessarily suggest, according to MacIver's own criterion, that the RPF was further to the left than the Socialist Party. If common sense rejects such an absurd proposition, so also does the logic of the election. The Communist Party, which received by far the largest proportion of the workers' vote, stood for a programme having far more in common with that of the Socialist Party than with that of the RPF. If, alternatively, MacIver would regard the Socialist Party as being to the left of the RPF, then the analysis would rest on a comparison of the *respective programmes* of the two parties and not on their records at the elections.

Once this principle of differentiation is admitted, we cannot

reason, as Lipset and Runciman do, that Peronism was a fascism of the Left because it won support from the lower classes. An analogy may be drawn to reinforce this point. Were the Italian peasants who in 1799 fought the Neapolitan Jacobins in the name of the Bourbons and the Holy Faith also part of a 'Rightism of the Left?' If so, was the same movement a 'Rightism of the Left' for the Bourbons themselves? Obviously not. Thus the same movement emerges, by this false approach, as being simultaneously a Rightism of the Left and a Rightism of the Right because peasants are supposedly 'left' and kings 'right'.

Clearly the adoption of a double standard, ideological and sociological, for defining the Left and Right leads only to the most appalling confusion. The truth is that if Peronism was in some senses a fascism of the Left it was because it offered a programme and policy which blended right- and left-wing elements. The left-

A procession of French trade unionists, May 1937. Their banner symbolises the unity of action between 'white-collar' and manual workers which was the basis of the Popular Front movement which the CGT supported.

wing elements happened to attract a large number of workers and peasants, but this is a factor quite irrelevant to the analysis. The left-wing programme of the French Socialist Party in 1951 did not in the event attract many workers and if the RPF gained more of the workers' votes it was self-evidently because those particular workers *were not attracted by a left-wing programme*. Lipset, we recall, spoke of Peronism being supported by the 'social strata who would otherwise turn to socialism or communism . . .'. This is an assumption on his part but it is a revealing assumption; for it is socialism and communism which are left-wing and not the social strata themselves.

Mr Runciman concedes that 'there are some political situations where to talk of Left and Right is wholly inappropriate or meaningless. This is the case for many periods even of Western European history.'[15] This is true. But have there not always existed rich and poor? If the sociological distinction between Left and Right is, as he maintains, 'the perennial argument between the poor and the rich', would it not follow that a Left and Right must have been 'perennially' in being?

All these writers have mistakenly identified the question for the answer. The question may be: when and where have the poor supported left-wing programmes? – which is quite different from concluding that the poor are the Left. We can ask where, when and why the Left or Right have secured the support of the different social classes only if we accept a single criterion – the political and ideological programme – as the basis for definition. Before we turn to the nature of this programme, one last fallacy must be examined.

A number of historians have been attracted by the idea that the Left stands for ' movement,' for opposition to the *status quo*. A basic dichotomy of the *parti de l'ordre établi* and the *parti de mouvement* as representing the cleavage between Right and Left in France has been formulated by Albert Thibaudet and later by François Goguel.[16] In 1955, the *Institut Français d'Opinion Publique* believed itself to have unearthed 'a fundamental difference between the man of the Left and the man of the Right. The first denounces the exist-

V.I. Lenin, the greatest of revolutionary leaders. Sometimes depicted as cruel and cynical, he was in fact an idealist fired by compassion for the under-privileged masses. Ruthless and pragmatic in his campaign to bring the Bolsheviks to power in Russia, he lacked both personal ambition and vanity. Lenin adapted Marxism to Russian conditions, declaring to his Menshevik-Marxist opponents: 'Revolution is not evolution'. Yet Marx had reasoned that it was.

ing state of things, while the second defends the established order.'

But the 'established order,' viewed either as an ideal or as a reality, defies any one description. The common distinction between 'reactionaries' and 'conservatives' suggests, after all, devotion to a previous *status quo* as opposed to the contemporary one. In France Legitimists and Orleanists, Bonapartists and conservative republicans have been unable to reach agreement as to the ideal *status quo*. Yet they constitute the essential French Right. Furthermore, to overthrow the present *status quo* in favour of a preferred one (as occurred in 1814 and 1830) represents movement. Fascism in opposition calls for change, for movement. The royalist exiles at Coblenz challenged the Jacobin 'established order' and the Tsarist Generals Kolchak and Wrangel challenged Lenin's, but they were not for that reason further to the left. The historians who have codified this law have confused movement with 'progress' and they have unduly narrowed their perspective by drawing their evidence from those long periods of French history when the 'established order' was as the Right, and not the Left, desired it.

Closely related to this error is a further one which insists that the more extreme the methods used in opposition to the *status quo*, the more left-wing the movement. G. D. H. Cole wrote that, 'after 1850 Marx had ceased to belong to the extreme Left of the revolutionary movement and had become acutely suspicious of mere *émeutisme* . . .'[17] Here leftism is measured by means rather than ends. The title of Lenin's *'Left Wing' Communism, an Infantile Disorder* (1920) brandishes a significant pair of inverted commas. We have as much reason as Lenin to doubt whether the extreme sectarians who refused to take part in parliamentary elections and whom he attacked on tactical grounds were in fact to the left of him. If the Left is to be distinguished from the Right by its programme, then obviously the extreme Left must be distinguished from the moderate Left also by its programme. There are a number of reasons why the extreme Left and the extreme Right alike very often tend to employ more violent methods than their moderate colleagues, but these methods are by-products of the extremism rather than its basis of definition.

2 Towards popular sovereignty

The French Revolution

The terms 'Left' and 'Right', as we pointed out earlier, are children of the French revolution, and this was not by accident. In the Constituent Assembly of 1789–91 there emerged four principal groupings which were inclined to shift their ground on each particular issue but which may be labelled the Right (Cazales, Maury), the Right Centre (*Les Monarchiens*), the Left Centre (Le Chapelier, Grégoire, Lafayette, Bailly), and the Extreme Left (Robespierre, Pétion de Villeneuve).

It was during the debates on the royal veto that the Assembly first divided into a Right, Centre and Left, representing respectively the demand for an absolute royal veto, a suspensive veto, and no veto at all. With regard to the structure of the legislature, the Right and Centre favoured an upper chamber whereas the Left Centre and the Left, who opposed any hereditary element, were associated with the demand for a single-chamber legislature. The Left and the Left Centre insisted that all power should lie with the elected assembly; the Right and Right Centre wanted the king to retain real power. The Centre – lacking though it did any firm personal or ideological cohesion – stood generally for the separation of powers among the various organs of government and administration, in the tradition of Montesquieu. But the Left, led by Robespierre, wished to minimise the power of the executive. The Right believed that judges should be dependent on the king; the Left called for judges elected by the people (even if instituted by the king) and for the power of the legislature to quash judicial decisions in the name of the people.

On the question of the franchise the Left separated totally not only from the Right but also from elements of the Left Centre and, at a later date, from the Girondins, or liberals. The existing franchise recognised a distinction between 'active' and 'passive' citizens, the latter enjoying only natural and civil rights, the former being endowed with the vote as well. The tax-paying qualification disfranchised nearly two out of six million adult males, and the remaining four million possessed only an indirect vote. Sieyès and

Condorcet approved of this type of limitation on the franchise but
Robespierre, Grégoire, Thibault and other leaders of the Left
continually challenged it in the Constituent Assembly.

On all these issues, the royal veto, the structure of the legislature,
the relative power of institutions, the judiciary and, above all, the
franchise, the Left adopted a position which had a single guiding
principle, a principle destined to become its hallmark for more than
a century-and-a-half – the demand for popular sovereignty. The
Jacobins, the members of the Jacobin Club and their supporters,
formed the spearhead of the Left, abolishing the old restricted
franchise and finally bringing themselves to power with popular
support. Further to the left, on the extreme Left, were certain
members of the Cordeliers Club and the disorganised *Enragés*, who
demanded absolute day-by-day popular control of the government and who challenged the Jacobin tendency towards dictatorial

centralisation. But the Left and extreme Left were more or less united in their struggle against the bourgeois liberals and the Girondins, who approved of the anti-aristocratic and anti-monarchical aspects of the revolution but who were deeply opposed to absolute democracy.

The Jacobins, of course, did not visualise popular sovereignty in terms of majority rule or latter-day parliamentary democracy. They were inspired by Rousseau's vision of the functioning of the social 'general will' and they shared, in principle at least, his aversion to representation of the people as tending inevitably to a perverted oligarchy. Robespierre distinguished between the 'representative of the people', who had no right to exist because 'the will cannot represent itself', and the preferable 'mandatory of the people, to whom the people has given the initial power'. This and some other of his claims, such as his desire to organise sovereignty 'in a manner equally removed from the tempests of absolute democracy and from the perfidious tranquillity of representative despotism,' may look remarkably like sophisms, whether taken in terms of their own internal contradictions or set beside Jacobin actions. But the sincerity of the underlying ideal is beyond question.

By 1793 the Left and extreme Left were in open conflict over the Jacobin aversion to what Robespierre called 'the tempests of absolute democracy.' The *Enragé* leader Varlet claimed in the name of the Parisian masses that, 'the electoral body of Paris is authorised to renew the members (of the Convention) who are traitors to the cause of the people . . .' On 4 May 1794, when a deputation from the faubourg Saint-Antoine arrived at the Convention, its spokesman called the bluff of the Jacobins when he claimed to speak on behalf of the 'members of the sovereign which has come to dictate its wishes to its mandatories'. Any proper delineation of the Left during the revolutionary period would include Robespierrists, Jacobins in general, Hébertists and *Enragés*; in other words, the Left in 1793 constituted those to the left of the Girondins. These groups were unified by one factor alone – their emphasis on popular sovereignty.

Camille Desmoulins making a speech at the Palais-Royal, by Daumier.
A much-admired revolutionary leader, Desmoulins died, alongside Danton and the
other 'indulgents', in Robespierre's final, self-defeating purge in April 1794.

Before 1789 the notion of popular sovereignty had been advocated by individual writers such as Winstanley and Rousseau, but it had not found expression in a mass movement at a national level. The franchise proposed in 1649 by the English Levellers, for example, would have extended to little more than one third of the potential male electorate. Most political situations, medieval or modern, reveal groups to the left of other groups, but the Left itself, viewed historically and conceptually, is an absolute based on a minimum demand of one man, one vote. Subsequent movements inspired by the French revolutionary democrats were not prepared to settle for less, and less, in any case, is not compatible with the concept of popular sovereignty. It follows that the Right, which emerged as the Right in the French Constituent Assembly by virtue of its opposition to the Left, is measurable as moderate or extreme to the extent of its denial of popular sovereignty.

If we regard the word 'advanced' in an historical rather than an ethical sense, we can safely say that Left and Right are manifestations of a society sufficiently advanced for the cause of popular sovereignty to be adopted by an effective national movement, but not yet advanced to the point of its final realisation.

In another and equally important sense, however, the Left is a dynamic force and has to be studied in terms of a dialectical progression of demand, concession and renewed demand. As Professor Micaud writes, 'the ideals proclaimed in 1789 carried promises for many that could not stop short of complete fulfilment in a classless society.' Put crudely, what was at first regarded as attainable by the transformation of political institutions came increasingly to be associated with the need for changes in the economic structure as well. One man, one vote, so the argument runs, achieves only a fake popular sovereignty so long as the means of production remain under private control. 'The wage-system,' wrote G. D. H. Cole, 'makes active citizenship impossible for the majority.' The 'new Left' which held this opinion came to maturity in the late nineteenth century. The predominantly political conception, satisfaction with universal suffrage or with direct popular control of the assemblies, which had been sufficient to distinguish the Left in 1792, was no longer so by 1914. The entire spectrum from Right to Left had moved to the left in the course of the nineteenth century, but a distinct Right and Centre continued to exist by virtue of their opposition to economic popular sovereignty and also by virtue of their hostility to certain institutional changes – such as the abolition of the French Senate – which would intensify popular control over government.

The classic movements of the old, political Left (although there were invariably economic aims as well) can be seen in the Jacobins, the Corresponding Societies, certain Benthamite radicals, the Chartists, Ledru-Rollin's Montagnards, the Mazzinians and the Jacksonian Democrats in America. But with writers and leaders such as Babeuf, his disciple Buonarroti, Blanc, Blanqui, O'Brien and of course Marx and Proudhon the economic Left evolved from the status of a sectarian minority to that of a dominant majority. 'Just as all citizens exercise political power in a democratic manner, in common,' said Jean Jaurès, the leader of the French Socialist Party, 'so they must exercise economic power in common as well.' In September 1942 the Resistance journal *Combat* declared: 'The revolution that we carry in us will be socialist because the time has come . . . to wrest from a powerful oligarchy the control and benefit of the economy, to restore to the nation or to the community of producers and consumers, as the case may be, important sectors of the economy.' And the historian Georges Lefebvre touched the heart of the new Left's ideology in drawing attention to 'a contradiction between the sovereignty of the people and universal suffrage on the one hand, placing the fate of the nation in the hands of everyone, and the capitalist economy where the wage-earner sees his work, his wages and consequently his life in the hands of those who own the means of production.'

The Left, then, has to be defined dynamically within its limited life-span both as a measure of its continuing separation from the Centre and Right and as an explanation of why the old, political Left, which refused to abandon its exclusively political approach to popular sovereignty, ceased at a certain stage to belong to the Left. I shall attempt later to suggest how this interesting phase of mutation and exclusion might be identified in a specific national context.

In emphasising that the Left is a dynamic or relative force it must at all costs be remembered that this relativism is restricted by an absolute criterion of one man, one vote. The common type of relativism which is so misleading is that which led to the parliamentary coalition which came to power in Italy in 1876 being called 'the Left.' In point of fact, the real Italian Left in the 1870's, the anarchists and the heirs of Mazzinian democracy and of Garibaldianism, was both small and far from the corridors of power. The so called Left of Depretis was in many ways more oppressive in its handling of the democrats than the so-called Right had been. By the law of 1882 ninety-three per cent of the potential electorate remained disfranchised.

The argument qualified

Before discussing the evolution of the Left in a particular historical context, a few qualifications must be made to the thesis as outlined so far, and some obvious objections perhaps answered.

There are a number of reasons why 'popular sovereignty' is preferable to 'democracy' as a term descriptive of the central creed of the Left. For the Ancients, democracy normally signified the rule of the *demos*, the populace or the poor, and was therefore a sectional form of government no less than oligarchy or aristocracy. Such a system has not appealed to the modern Left. Lenin, Trotsky, Rosa Luxemburg and other Marxists have, it is true, regarded 'democracy' in a somewhat analogous light, as the rule of workers and peasants over all other classes, but this state of affairs they regarded as purely provisional and not as an ultimate ideal. Nor has the more typical version of democracy through parliamentary representation emerged as universally acceptable to the Left. Robespierre held that no man could represent another and Proudhon wrote that '*le suffrage universel est à mes yeux une vraie lotterie*'. Finally, the fact cannot be ignored that Marxists, anarchists and syndicalists have all regarded government under any form as incompatible with absolute popular sovereignty, and democracy, in any of its variants, is a form of government. A recent historian of the anarchist movement, Mr Woodcock, in arguing that 'Democracy advocates the sovereignty of the people. Anarchism advocates the sovereignty of the person,'[18] thereby seems to identify sovereignty of the people with government by the people. It is certainly not unreasonable to do so; if the anarchist condition represents a power vacuum, then sovereignty as such might be said to have vanished from the social scene. But it can equally be argued that sovereignty merely signifies control, the possession of ultimate power, and not the exercise of that power through government. To abolish government is in itself an act of sovereignty; if the people are not sovereign they will not succeed in establishing anarchism or in maintaining it, as was seen during the Spanish Civil War.

It may be asked: to what extent is popular sovereignty an end in itself, and to what extent only a means to an end? Briefly, it is both. The notion of self-government is a single manifestation, albeit the primary one, of a wider egalitarian impulse. But we have already discovered that the desire for equality is too vague and ambiguous a formula to provide a satisfactory definition of the Left. The only connecting link between all left-wing ideals of equality, from Jacobins to anarchists, is that of popular sovereignty, and it is the degree of popular sovereignty envisaged as feasible or desirable by the Left at any given time which provides the insight into the degree of equality envisaged. The Jacobins, for example, did not expect all inequalities of wealth and ownership to disappear and so they stopped short of advocating popular control of the economy. That subjectively at least popular sovereignty and equality have been regarded by the Left as two faces of the same coin is well brought out by Clause Four of the British Labour Party Constitution of 1918, which pledged the Party to secure 'for the workers by hand or by brain the full fruits of their industry and the most equitable distribution thereof that may be possible, upon the basis of the common ownership of the means of production and the best obtainable system of popular administration and control of each industry . . .'

There is of course, no certainty that the people, endowed with sovereignty over any particular sphere, will exercise that sovereignty to any predictable end, egalitarian or otherwise. It is also true that some left-wing leaders, the nineteenth-century revolutionist Auguste Blanqui being the most conspicuous, have concluded that the people can be expected to value their sovereignty and advance towards equality only after a period of enlightenment and education. Here we come upon the problem of the left 'authoritarians' and of the Jacobin and Bolshevik dictatorships under which the sovereignty of the people, or even of the lower classes, was more nominal than real. It would, however, be wrong to conclude automatically that the agents of dictatorship had ceased to be of the Left. Political actions have to be judged in a context of opposing forces and not in a vacuum. The question is, did the Jacobins (or Lenin) genuinely believe that the war against the enemies of popular sovereignty demanded for the sake of efficiency a provisional dictatorship which would disappear once the crisis period had passed? Robespierre and Lenin clearly ended their political lives as they had begun them, as men of the Left. But with every passing year of non-democratic rule motives become increasingly difficult to assess; the contradiction presented by the Stalinist Constitution of 1936, almost a model for popular democracy, and the unprecedented police terror and state of oppression, is difficult to solve.

Application of the model

Having constructed an outline model of the Left we may return to the partisan statement quoted earlier that 'by any strict use of language Liberals are the true Left, the real progressives'. The motive for rejecting the assertion is not a partisan one; the mainstream of European liberalism does not coincide with the model.

The French revolution provided three main models which corresponded to the three main trends of the post-Restoration opposition in the era of absolutist monarchies: the moderate liberal (the Girondins), the radical democratic (the Jacobins), and the socialist (the Babouvists). Of these, the moderate liberals alone were not of the Left. Not until late in the nineteenth century and early in the twentieth did the majority of liberals accept the principle of universal suffrage. Benjamin Constant, the leading theorist of the more enlightened post-Restoration liberalism, was convinced that 'the abstract recognition of popular sovereignty does not augment in anything the sum of the liberties of the individual.' The question for Constant was how to limit sovereignty *per se*. In fact he shared with other liberals of his time an implacable hatred of democracy. Although the extensions of the franchise in France and Britain in 1830 and 1832 did not satisfy all liberals (particularly in France), their quarrel was more with the limitations of the extension than with the principle of limitation itself. The German liberals were on the whole even less inclined to regard democracy with anything but horror. John Stuart Mill, despite his sympathy for the poor and economically exploited, advocated an allocation of votes in proportion to merits and a second chamber of the best minds. For him, as for Tocqueville, the rule of the masses was bound to militate against liberty and enlightenment. Cobden and the Manchester school were all for individual opportunity but this, as their staunch opposition to the Chartists showed, did not imply universal suffrage. Liberals have on the whole been to the left of conservatives and Lloyd George's battle with the House of Lords was leftist in the sense that it operated in the direction of political popular sovereignty, but the Asquith government nevertheless failed to introduce universal suffrage in the most economically advanced country in Europe.

Benjamin Constant's fears have not been forgotten by later liberal theorists, although the objection to democracy has been discarded for one reason or another. Liberalism has been transformed in the course of a century and a half but it retains a characteristic refusal to make of sovereignty the fundamental social question. When an English liberal economist writes that 'most of the social tensions surviving in Britain today are due to the unequal distribution of property,' one observes how far his emphasis differs from that of the socialist Pierre Mendès-France who writes that 'in an advanced economy the motor must be popular pressure, the will of the people educated in advance to play the role . . . freedom and efficacy will finally be reconciled and associated.'

This is naturally not to say that the Left has no concern with the distribution of property or that it does not consider the exercise of sovereignty to be as important as its attainment. Many of the major economic struggles between Left and Right have related only indirectly to the issue of sovereignty, through a demand for greater equality. The introduction, for example, of a graduated income tax is an end in itself but it also affects the balance of sovereignty for two reasons: firstly, its enactment reflects the growing power of the masses, and power is a prelude to sovereignty; secondly, and more important, the effect of the tax would be to weaken and diminish sectional wealth and consequently its power to obstruct the realisation of popular sovereignty in the economic or political spheres. The total aggregate of such legislation largely accounts for the movement of the entire political spectrum to the left in the course of a century and a half.

If the conclusion that the mainstream of liberalism has not formed an integral part of the European Left is not an altogether surprising one, the application of the model to certain marginal cases – in this instance the Utopian socialists Owen and Saint-Simon – results in a more radical reversal of accepted perspectives. For these two pioneers of socialist thought, praised by Marx and Engels, were not in fact men of the Left.

In 1817 Robert Owen attacked what he called the 'premature reformists.' In propagating his theories he was keen to gain the ear of men in power and enjoyed the friendship of the Tory leaders Liverpool, Sidmouth and Castlereagh. In September 1832, the *Poor Man's Guardian* complained that the Owenites sought 'every opportunity to speak sneeringly and contemptuously' of political

Robert Owen's utopian socialism in practice.
A view of one of the settlements he founded at Orbiston.
It lasted only two years. Although a socialist,
Owen was not strictly a man of the Left;
he was a paternalist and educator, without faith in
popular self-government.

rights. In general Owen was opposed to any elements whose activities might increase social strife, and in 1848 he denounced 'Red Republicans, Communists and Socialists of Europe' whose principles led to 'universal disunion, opposition, competition . . . a pandemonium state of society.' Seven years later he reflected that, 'it has always been my impression . . . that it will be much easier to reform the world through Governments, properly supported by the people, than by any other means.' Owen in fact disapproved of the entire revolutionary movement, democratic and socialist, which swept Europe in 1848. The essential point is not that Owen liked to work through governments (Lassalle and the Fabians were later attracted by the same tactic) but rather that he rejected the direct intervention of the masses in politics and government. In contrast, his admirer William Thompson was a socialist *of the Left* because he was a democrat who advocated a system of provincial, state and national legislatures elected by the people, with judges and all officials also appointed on the basis of popular election.

Similarly, Henri de Saint-Simon, who at one stage appealed to

Jean-Paul Marat, one of the fiercest of the left-wing Jacobin leaders. His paper, *Ami du Peuple*, was popular among the Parisian sans-culottes. Following the purge of the Girondins in 1793, Marat was murdered in his bath as an act of political retribution.

Napoleon to bring into being his rational social system, admired none of the heroes of the revolution and had no patience with popular sovereignty. The people, he argued, possessed neither the knowledge nor the leisure to be sovereign 'except in moments of brief delirium'. Life under the Jacobin-dominated Convention had been 'complete anarchy'. He, like Owen, was an apostle of 'reason'; questions of sovereignty were to be condemned as emanating from the realm of passion and narrow self-interest. It is hardly surprising that Owen and the Owenites and Saint-Simon and the Saint-Simonians were bitterly challenged by the democrats in England and France. The Saint-Simonians made no impact on the labour movement while the Owenites who joined the Chartists did so at the cost of abandoning an important element in their master's teaching.

The old and new Lefts: France

It remains to examine under what circumstances the old, political Left ultimately gives way to the new, economic Left and so ceases to be of the Left. French, English, German and Italian history suggest in each case a slightly different pattern of evolution, but for reasons of space the French case alone can be discussed here in sufficient detail to indicate how the conceptual model may be applied to a specific situation.

The predominantly economic Left (Babeuf, Buonarroti, Blanc, Blanqui, Proudhon) existed as a junior partner to the predominantly political Left (Marat, Robespierre, Hébert, Ledru-Rollin, Lamartine, Delescluze, Rochefort) from the time of the revolution until the Paris Commune of 1871. But until political popular sovereignty in its minimum form had been established beyond challenge, the Jacobins and their Radical successors remained, in accordance with the dialectic of the demand and the reality, an integral part of the French Left. The transitional phase during which this contradiction was finally resolved through a series of marked advances and partial regressions occupied a span of rather more than thirty years and began on the eve of the Franco-Prussian war of 1870.

Thirty republican deputies had been elected to the Imperial legislature in 1869. Less concerned with economic and labour problems than were Varlin, Malon and the other leaders of the French section of the First International, they all stood for universal suffrage and democratic government. Léon Gambetta declared in his Belleville Manifesto that 'for those who believe that the People is the one lawful sovereign, and must really exercise power, mere responsibility of ministers to parliament is not enough . . .'

The deputies returned by Paris in the elections to the National Assembly in February 1871 were, despite Louis Blanc's socialist past, Rochefort's editorship of the extremist *L'Intransigeant* and Delescluze's commitment to the Commune, essentially men of the political Left. By July 1871, there were in the Assembly 350 republicans whose objective position, in view of the precarious and uncodified life of the new Republic, was a left-wing one. But after 1877, when the republican Left overcame the challenge of MacMahon's dissolution of the Assembly, the resulting stabilisation led to realignments and, for the historian, a reappraisal of the frontiers of the Left.

The victory of the old Left in the elections of 1881, and particularly of Ferry's *Gauche républicaine* and Gambetta's *Union républicaine*, followed by a period of moderate republican administration, brought about a situation whereby these elements became content, despite their anti-clerical measures, with the extent of popular sovereignty already achieved, and so dropped out of the Left. For the *Gauche républicaine*, as for the *Centre gauche* (Say, Renault, Casimir-Périer) the Republic '*serait conservatrice ou ne serait pas*'. Those who like Clemenceau now constituted the political Left were demanding the suppression of the Senate and Presidency, separation of Church and State, the substitution of a militia for the standing army, the election of judges, divorce, a progressive income tax, reduction of the working day, the abolition of the *livret ouvrier* – an extension of the Montagnard platform of 1848 with its slogan of '*vive la République démocratique et sociale*'. Clemenceau's programme contained social elements but it was not socialist; its emphasis was political when compared with those of Jules Guesde's Marxist *Parti ouvrier*, of Paul Brousse's 'Possibi-

lists' and of the Allemanists. For some years a distinct political
Left existed in the Chamber of Deputies composed firstly of a group
not more than sixty in number in the years 1885–9 and not less than
thirty-six in number in the Chamber of 1889–93, and, secondly, to
their immediate right, of the *Radicaux de Gauche*, about twenty-five
strong on average. They championed labour's right to strike and,
after the legislation of 1884, they tended to defend the trade unions
against both hostile employers and ministries. But years of republican power gradually eroded the left-wing element among the
Radicals. The rise of the socialist groups, of collectivism and militant syndicalism, weakened the sentimental appeal of the slogan 'no
enemies to the left.'

It was the conjunction of the latent anti-republican threat posed
by the Church and the dwindling monarchist party and periodic
crises such as the Boulanger and Dreyfus affairs which kept a substantial proportion of the anti-socialist democrats objectively on
the Left. A more or less united political and economic Left triumphed; for a few years the mystique of the Dreyfusard Left remained
intact and Combes, who became Premier in 1902, was no less committed than was Jaurès to the parliamentary *Délégation des
Gauches* which influenced the government's actions until 1905.

1905 provides a dividing line. The dominant issues were no longer
constitutional or ecclesiastical but social and economic. Despite the
existence of a Senate elected on an indirect franchise and favouring
the rural community, demands for the extension of popular sovereignty were henceforward directed towards the economic sphere.
The Socialist Party in parliament and the syndicalist *Confédération
Général du Travail* (CGT) in the streets and factories went into
permanent opposition.

The Radicals were reluctant to acknowledge the logic of the
situation. They operated mainly under the title *Parti Radical-
Socialiste* and they were attracted periodically by electoral alliances
such as the *Cartel des Gauches* (1924) and the *Front populaire*
(1935). But they did not co-operate with the socialists in 1919 and
they parted company with them soon after the electoral victories of

1924, 1932 and 1936. By 1926 Radical deputies were supporting the right-wing Poincaré administration; the electoral alliance of 1932 was immediately belied when the Radical Herriot, on forming a government, rejected the socialist conditions for participation and when subsequently he, Paul-Boncour and Daladier were overthrown because of their refusal to make the concessions which might have secured socialist co-operation. It is a mistake made by more than one historian to identify the opposition to the *Cartel des Gauches* with the Centre and the Right. Electoral labels were artificial and misleading; the Centre began in fact within the *Cartel*, with the Radical Party.

The growth of the extreme right-wing Leagues and the riots of 6 February 1934 presented a revived threat to the Republic, to political popular sovereignty itself, and so brought the Radicals back temporarily into an objectively left-wing position. But it was not long after the Popular Front victory of 1936 that they began to reveal again their hostility to an extension of popular sovereignty and to greater equality in the industrial sphere. The fatal defiance of Blum by the Senate in June 1937 reflected the courage that Caillaux and other Radicals had taken from the new Employers' Federation's defiant attitude towards the Matignon wage agreements and collective bargaining. On 7 April 1938, the Radicals in the Senate rejected the demand of the second Blum government for a tax on capital. At the end of 1938 the Radical National Congress formally quit the Popular Front.

After the Liberation, the Radicals, under Herriot's leadership, opposed the constitutional projects of the two Constituent Assemblies which were supported by the socialists and communists and designed to increase the measure of direct popular sovereignty. A small group, the *Radicaux de Gauche*, left the Party in disgust. Even Mendès-France, who stood to the left of the Party, was not identifiable as a member of the French Left until his conversion to socialism and to the PSU. As Premier he wanted to modernise the economy and centrally orientate investment, provide cheap credit for agriculture and eliminate marginal enterprises. But a New Deal is one thing and the Left another. The Gaullist régime also emphasises technocratic planning. What distinguishes the Left is not its addiction to planning but its insistence on popular control and participation.

The Left today

What at first sight may seem to complicate any attempt to delineate the contemporary Left is the increasing intrusion of the problem of means to an end. Although the state socialists had been divided from anarchists and syndicalists on this question from an early date, the full complexity of the problem became apparent only after the Left in Russia, and to a lesser extent in western Europe, encountered the practical obstacles to the achievement of popular control of the economy. G. D. H. Cole wrote: 'the community must interfere in industry, and, ultimately, control; and the question . . . is . . . the best method of exercising that control.'

Faced with the problem, one section of the Left came to respect the Keynesian or mixed economy. The Frankfurt Declaration of the Socialist International in 1952 stated that socialist planning 'does not presuppose public ownership of all the means of production . . .'. The Social Democratic Parties have committed themselves to the acceptance of a mixed economy, often in its present form. Does it therefore follow, as Raymond Aron has argued, that there now exists a Keynesian, anti-Malthusian Left and a quite distinct anti-capitalist Left?

An authentic Keynesian Left is possible only in a situation where the extent of political popular sovereignty leaves much to be desired. The Fifth French Republic may constitute such a situation; there may be Keynesians who believe that its structure thwarts the popular will. But in general a Keynesian Left is a contradiction in terms, a myth fostered by the acceptance of the present balance of economic sovereignty by a large section of the European socialist movement. While it is not difficult to demonstrate that the Whigs did not constitute the eighteenth-century British Left, and that the

Left cannot be defined on a relative basis alone, the feeling persists that in our own day there must be a Left and that any party calling itself socialist must be an integral part of it. But to admit this would be to deny the whole historical logic of the analysis. Once a movement becomes content with adjusting checks and balances, with redistributions, and once it has ceased to attempt to extend the frontiers of popular sovereignty, it has abandoned the dynamic of the Left. At a certain stage the French Radical Party ceased to be left-wing; more recently the right wings of the Socialist and Labour Parties have done likewise. Today the Left generally begins at some point *within* these Parties.

To accept this analysis is to accept why the Left cannot at any time be equated simply with sympathy for the oppressed, optimism, liberty and the other enduring ideals. But if we measure these ideals against the yardstick of popular sovereignty – of which they are obviously more the parents than the children – it becomes clearer why they, in one form or another, have been remarkably in evidence on the Left. Popular sovereignty signifies at least the *liberty* to a voice in public affairs, to a share in the control of one's own destiny; the *equality* of men in so far as they all enjoy this liberty and are likely to use it to achieve a wider measure of social and economic equality; a certain *optimism* about men's ability to govern themselves; *rationalism* in the sense that it denies metaphysically derived sources of authority such as Divine Right; *antimilitarism* by analogy, for if the people of one nation can attain sufficient harmony to distribute sovereignty among themselves, then surely the different nations can also learn to regulate their differences peacefully; *sympathy for the oppressed* in so far as it puts them within reach of changing their own condition; *social reform* because a sovereign people could hardly avoid reforming the society over which they had previously not been sovereign and because the long-term effect of the totality of social reforms is, whatever their intention, to increase popular sovereignty; and finally *movement* because this insistent demand has proved to be the most dynamic force for change in modern European history.

PART TWO

Ends and means

3 The early years

1789–1848

The French revolution, the first of the great physical clashes between Left and Right at both a national and an international level, like the Spanish Civil War, one of the last, imposed on a Europe for whom the rumblings of a second, industrial eruption were already audible a profoundly schismatic crisis. The Jacobins, like Luther, had declared, 'Here I stand!' They could not be ignored.

French democratic republicanism was home-grown, born from the logic of the struggles of 1789–92. Serious philo-Jacobinism and pro-French feeling was manifest mainly in the areas adjoining France, the Low Countries, the Rhineland, Switzerland, Savoy and Italy, and to some extent in Poland and Ireland. In Britain – or rather in the British government – was to be found in the inflexibly self-interested enemy of the revolution and of the Napoleonic Empire that followed it. But England was not without its sympathisers and fellow-travellers. The London Corresponding Society, founded in 1792, attracted to its ranks democrats like John Thelwall and Horne Tooke, rebels who made contact with the French Convention, of which Thomas Paine even became a member. The embryonic British Left was divided over the Terror; of the few who supported it unreservedly, Thomas Hardy was the most notable. Subjectively and objectively, both in their view of society and in society's view of them, these men played a role not unlike that of the West European communists in the 1920's, isolated apologists for a régime commonly regarded as a denial of civilisation itself. The Corresponding Society, suppressed as subversive in 1799, acted as a sort of seminary for the left-wing agitators of the period which closed with the abortive Cato Street Conspiracy. Its mission was taken up in the provinces by the Hampden Clubs whose central demands were for manhood suffrage and the repeal of the Combination Acts which made trade unionism illegal.

Although Jacobinism and Bonapartism made some headway in Italy as modernising, anti-feudal forces, the post-Napoleonic Carbonari, or Secret Societies, were not generally democratic and

Caricature of Louis Philippe by Daumier.
Following the overthrow of
the last Bourbon king in July 1830,
the moderate conservative Louis Philippe
soon turned against the republicans and
democrats who had helped to bring him to power.

it was not until Giuseppe Mazzini founded *Young Italy* at Marseilles in July 1831 that the Italian Left found its progenitor. For forty years the most coherent exponent of a unified, republican and democratic Italy, Mazzini proclaimed the ideal nation to be 'the totality of citizens speaking the same language associated together with equal political and civil rights . . .' But in his lifetime he was to remain frustrated.

Further afield in Tsarist Russia, the Jacobin flame flickered briefly, perhaps anachronistically, when the 'Decembrist' rebels, a group of officers of the Guard, attempted in December 1825 a *coup* which was part revolution and part palace *putsch*. The northern rebels were constitutionalists rather than democrats, but in the

48

South Pavel Ivanovich Pestel staked his claim (and his life) to become the pioneer of the Russian political Left by calling for manhood suffrage, a centralised and democratic republic, the emancipation of the serfs, and their endowment with half the land of Russia. The Decembrists failed, but thirty years later, when a new Russian Left emerged, the peasants were still the principal objects of its compassion.

If the British Reform Bill of 1832 satisfied a section of the liberal and vote-hungry middle class, among the lower orders it stimulated disillusionment with constitutional agitation and indeed with the whole parliamentary apparatus. The National Union of the Working Classes and its organ, *The Poor Man's Guardian*, edited by the future Chartist leader Bronterre O'Brien, represented, or contained, perhaps the first revolutionary syndicalist movement, the first of many subsequent working-class rejections of the political kingdom in favour of the industrial. When the movement collapsed in 1834, dragging down with it the labour exchanges and co-operative societies, it left the ground fallow for Chartism and a return to political methods of persuasion.'

The Chartists were democrats and they operated on a national scale. Their main aims were embodied in the famous 'six points': universal male suffrage, equal electoral districts, removal of the property qualification for MP's, payment of MP's, secret ballot, and annual general elections. (The first five of these demands were granted between 1858 and 1918, but the sixth has been regarded as impracticable.) There had been no analogous movement in Britain since the Levellers of the 1640's, and there was to be none again until the rise of the Independent Labour Party in the 1890's. The Chartists' 'six points' implied, as their Tory, Whig and Liberal opponents were quick to appreciate, a very real sovereignty of the people in the political sphere. Whereas the Jacobins, at least in theory, went in search of '*la volonté générale*', the Chartists tapped an English tradition in claiming justification for their demands in natural law; their leaders Lovett, O'Brien and O'Connor frequently invoked the law of nature, but their insight into the social basis of

laws and institutions was not so obtuse as some have supposed, and O'Brien and Harney, in any case, derived a wider perspective from their reading of the Jacobin leaders Marat and Robespierre. The Charter, the great petition signed by millions of people (and signed by some many times over) subsumed local and specific subsidiary demands such as factory and currency reform, abolition of the new poor law and of the corn laws. Democracy suddenly appeared as the indispensable key to every avenue of advancement.

The British Left in the 1830's discovered its right wing within the camp of rationalist radicals whose schoolmaster had been the utilitarian, and latterly democrat, philosopher Jeremy Bentham. In December 1837, the Birmingham Political Union somewhat reluctantly decided to sublimate its propaganda for fiscal reform in the demand for manhood suffrage, and in June 1839 its leader Thomas Attwood presented the Chartist Petition to Parliament, supported by forty-six MP's – the Parliamentary Left. But the Chartists made little headway within the political nation from which the majority of their supporters were debarred; by May 1842 the number of MP's voting in support of the Charter had grown by only three.

The Chartists and the middle class radicals were no less divided in temper and tempo than were the moderate and extreme democrats in contemporary France. The London Working Men's Association complained in 1837 of those 'who call themselves Radicals' but few of whom 'are truly representatives of the wants and wishes of the producing classes.' By the end of 1842, some fifty or sixty Suffrage Unions had appeared in the industrial centres and a national Complete Suffrage Movement led by Joseph Sturge had separated itself from the most vocal and influential pressure group of the anti-democratic bourgeoisie, the Anti-Corn Law League. But while Sturge and his friends spoke up for manhood suffrage, they were far from accepting all the six points of the Charter. There was in fact a basic incompatibility between the somewhat self-satisfied rationalism of the middle class radicals and the incoherent yet passionate aspirations of the workers. The Chartists, like the Mazzinians in Italy, were to be frustrated in their lifetime.

The minor electoral advance of 1832 took the form of a constitutional evolution. There was pressure and sometimes violence in the great towns, but the issue was decided in Parliament. By way of contrast, the July Monarchy in France was the beneficiary of the revolutionary tradition set in motion in 1789; the eminently bourgeois Louis Philippe owed his throne to the barricades. But Orleanism, no less conscious than British liberalism that the many had triumphed against the few on the backs of the multitude, was no less eager to proclaim that enough was enough, no less willing to transform guilt into physical oppression, no less prepared to create a paradise for finance capitalists and speculators. One Frenchman in 200 now had the vote. The two-score-and-six who upheld the Charter in Parliament were few enough, but they were a multitude when set beside the solitary Garnier-Pagès whose speeches represented the voice of republicanism in the French Chamber in the 1830's. An organised Republican Party failed to mature. Under the premiership of Casimir Périer papers were seized, democrats were put on trial and in 1834 the *Société des Droits de l'Homme* succumbed to a purge that would have done credit to the Bourbons.

After 1840, 'utopian' schemes fell into disrepute as it dawned on socialists and communists that if they stood for the salvation of the masses they could do worse than turn to them for support. At the same time, hardly able to credit that monarchism could ever be liquidated, left-wing writers turned to history for confirmation, tracing the schism between bourgeois constitutionalism and popular democracy to the conflict between Voltaire and Rousseau, between Girondins and Jacobins. The words and actions of Marat and Robespierre were circulated quietly in the *ateliers* of Paris as models to be imitated in a not-too-distant future. In 1848 the pattern of 1830 was to be repeated. The democratic middle class, also riding on the backs of the multitude, had their way and the monarchy fell. But by June 1848, when the desperate workers of Paris were shot down in their hundreds, the middle classes too had decided that enough is enough.

From Germany, less industrialised than France and feudal in contrast to England, the Left received a unique gift at this period, the gift of brilliantly schematic minds determined to destroy the moral and utopian foundations of socialism. The German states produced a generation of communist exiles, among them Wilhelm Weitling who discovered in French experience a unique synthesis of his own – socialist utopianism, insistence that the workers must act on their own behalf, and faith in an élitist *coup* – and also Moses Hess from whom Engels first learned his communism.

That the dialectic – movement based on the constant resolution of conflicts – represented the fundamental law of historical progression was an assumption that Karl Marx shared with a generation of young Germans who had learned their philosophy under the shadow of the most complex of system-builders, Hegel. The assumption itself had a relative, if not an absolute bias towards the Left in the sense that it challenged the sanctity of the *status quo* which was at that time generally the preserve of the Right. If Hegel had latterly come to revere the Prussian monarchy, it was at the cost, as many of his disciples realised, of arbitrarily freezing the dialectic. For Hegel the dialectic operated in the realm of the Idea, the Spirit; Marx transferred the dialectic to the realm of matter, at the same time combatting the 'mechanical' materialism which posits man as the passive receptacle of an unchanging natural order. Men, he insisted, make their own history. A determinist, convinced that history had a predictable outcome, he thought in terms of historical necessity, defining freedom by its dialectical relationship to necessity. Thus the masses would fight for freedom because they must, because capitalism would inevitably impoverish them in an ever greater degree, and because they must they would choose to do so. 'The philosophers have only interpreted the world in various ways; the point is to change it.' For Marx, scientific philosophy, that is to say Marxism, became a material force in transforming, or in aiding the proletariat to transform, the present into the future. Ostensibly opposed to all moralism, he fashioned a convenient monism of being and ought-to-be, while revealing with every line he wrote his underlying moral indignation at the suffering of the masses.

In September 1847, the radicals of Baden, in Germany, drew up the Offenburg programme of left-wing democracy. But their differences with the moderates could not be papered over. In a Konrad Heinzen, a Lamartine, a Mazzini, a Sturge, the distrust of European democracy for socialism was plainly evident. The moderate socialists of eastern Germany like Stephan Born enjoyed more success in 1848–9 than the Rhineland extremists, but even their followers did not exceed 12,000. The middle classes were terrified of the 'spectre haunting Europe' – communism, the barbarian masses rising from their slumber. It was the soldiers' brutality in Berlin that turned agitation spontaneously into insurrection on 18 March 1848, leading to a series of bloodless *coups* in central Germany and to rapid advances on the democratic front. But in Germany, as elsewhere, concessions were illusory so long as the social balance of forces remained to the Left's disadvantage, so long as the middle classes feared the masses more than the old régime. The revolutions of 1848, which will be discussed in a different context, served only as a prelude to a new era of conservative stabilisation. By 1851 the people were nowhere sovereign.

The First and Second Internationals

The foundation in 1864 of the First International, the International Working Men's Association (IWMA), revealed at once not only the enduring rift between the moderate and extreme Lefts but also a dangerous tendency to fragmentation within the new, economic Left. The various doctrines, Marxist, collectivist, reformist, anarchist and mutualist, which had developed in comparative isolation during the period of conservative hegemony, now experienced for the first time a direct confrontation. Neither concession nor synthesis was forthcoming; temporary compromises and the agreement to differ were the best that could be hoped for.

The IWMA, which grew out of contacts established between British and French trade union leaders, and to which individuals rather than parties were affiliated (the total membership claimed in 1870 being 800,000), made considerable headway in Belgium and Switzerland while achieving minor penetrations in Italy, Spain and Germany. Marx, for whom the primary objective was to root his doctrine in the broadest possible strata of the labour movement after more than a decade of scholarly seclusion in England, was at once faced with the dominance of Proudhon's co-operative movement in France and of Lassalle's variety of socialism in Germany, the one as absurd in his eyes as the other was pernicious. No sooner had Marxism begun to make headway, profiting from the deaths of Lassalle and Proudhon in 1864 and 1865, than a new but equally influential challenge appeared in the shape of Bakunin, the apostle of anarchist collectivism, of the immediate destruction of government and the state. 'This Russian,' Marx wrote to Engels in 1869, 'wants to become the dictator of the European workers' movement.' In 1872 he managed to have the anarchists expelled, but by then, following the collapse of the Paris Commune, the IWMA was itself a spent force capable only of self-liquidation.

The Paris Commune of March 1871, the revolutionary passion-play of the nineteenth-century working class, national in its immediate preoccupations but international in implication, was all things to all men. Guided by a Jacobin-Blanquist majority and a few members of the IWMA, yet with a Proudhonist emphasis on federalism, on a federation of semi-autonomous communes throughout France, it could at the same time be regarded as nothing more than a democratically-elected municipal government. A unique fusion of doctrinaire agitation and pragmatic action, its defeat in a trial of strength was a set-back that shattered the international cohesion (precarious as it had been) of the extreme Left, which was to remain atomised in its national components until the foundation of the Second International in 1889.

The Second International inherited the schisms and the legacy of bitterness that had marred the First. When two rival Congresses met, one Marxist and the other organised by the French 'Possibilist' Paul Brousse, representing the two dominant trends within the state-socialist school, confusion complemented animosity. The anarchists, who at once raised a rumpus pleasing neither to Marxists nor 'Possibilists,' were at first conciliated, then chastised and finally, in 1896, expelled. Marxism, which had until the late 1880's held sway in Germany alone, was now coming into its own

at an international level, more visionary and idealistic than reformism and more coherent and realistic than the abstentionist currents of anarchism and syndicalism. As a fully developed theory of action, it owed most to Engels, Kautsky and Plekhanov; as an action based on theory, its key leaders were Liebknecht and Bebel in Germany, Guesde in France and Victor Adler in Austria. Not till much later did Lenin, who was to put both theory and action on a new basis and in so doing was to inflict a lethal injury on the Second International, become at all widely known.

That the new, economic Left came to maturity in the last quarter of the nineteenth century is reflected in the rapid proliferation of Socialist Parties, generally with a Marxist basis, within the space of a decade and a half; in Germany in 1875; in France and Spain in 1879; in Britain in 1884; in Norway in 1887; in Austria and Switzerland in 1888; in Sweden and Holland in 1889; in Italy, Poland and Finland in 1892. If none was identical in structure or doctrine with another, they nevertheless presented in conjunction, as members of the Second International, a threat to political stability which governments could not ignore.

Two victories for reaction.
Above: the Milanese erect barricades against Austrian rule
in 1848 – their freedom was short-lived.
Below: Porte Maillot, Paris, 1871, after the revolutionary
Commune had fallen to Thiers' national army.

4 Adolescence and maturity

Western Europe, 1848–1914

Although the collapse of Chartism in 1848 did not extinguish the suffrage movement in Britain, it did have the effect of channelling working-class aspirations, particularly those of the skilled workers enjoying the sunlight of mid-Victorian prosperity, into trade unionism, the rewards of which seemed more concrete and more immediate. But radicalism was not dead. In the mood of bourgeois self-congratulation which followed the repeal of the corn laws in 1846 the curious notion that England ought to be a democracy was not entirely lost sight of. John Bright's proposal for a limited extension of the franchise to all rate-payers was rejected in 1858 as insufficiently radical by Suffrage Associations in Manchester, York, Rochdale and elsewhere. In the 1860's, with the affiliation of certain trade unionists to the IWMA and with the appearance of the Labour Representation League, a working-class Left began to emerge once more.

The Labour movement, at first a satellite of the Liberal Party, began to move into independent orbit in the late 1880's, when Keir Hardie remarked intransigently; 'if the Liberal Party desires to prevent a split, let it adopt the programme of the Labour Party.' Some, particularly among the older, more established trade unions and among the Labour representatives in Parliament known as 'Lib-Labs', doubted the efficacy of this policy, and their fears seemed confirmed in 1895 when not a single Independent Labour Party (ILP) candidate was elected. Beatrice Webb reflected in her diary: 'the ILP has completed its suicide.' The judgment was premature.

Real though the organic connection with the Liberal Party was, the claim made by Ramsay MacDonald in his *Socialism and Society* that, 'socialism, the stage which follows liberalism, retains everything of permanent value that was in liberalism . . .'. was quite false. Organisation is one thing and ideology another. Ideologically, socialism follows everywhere from democratic radicalism, the extreme Left from the moderate Left. Liberalism and the Left pursue parallel lines, in mutual contradiction. The motive of MacDonald, Hardie, Glasier and other Labour spokesmen for insisting on a doctrinal connection lay in their repugnance against the Marxist stress on class war and in their insistence that socialism was a moral force, the result of ethical progress. But the programme of the Labour Party had far more in common with Marxism than with liberalism. The first meeting of the ILP at Bradford in 1891 passed by a large majority a resolution calling for the 'collective ownership of the means of production, distribution and exchange,' and in 1918 – to leap ahead – the Labour Party advocated the immediate nationalisation of land, railways, mines, electricity, industrial insurance, harbours and so forth, as well as the extension of social services and education on the basis of a steeply progressive income tax. Marxist categories and the Marxist teleology were adopted while Marxist means of combat tended to be rejected.

British history affords no better example of the fusion of largely Marxist purposes with gradualist methods than the Fabian Society, founded in 1884. The Fabians, who inherited and adapted Bentham's utilitarianism, saw in collectivist socialism the logical extension of Benthamite radicalism. But there were differences. Whereas Bentham had been inclined to view society as a kind of roof supported by weak vertical pillars (law, organisation, religion, etc.), the Fabians, less abstract because more class-conscious, saw instead a horizontal structure, with the bottom floor composed of producers and the top floor populated by a powerful oligarchy. Bentham wanted political democracy; the Fabians wanted economic democracy as well; both relied on 'piece-meal social engineering' to achieve their chosen aims.

The Fabians grew away from the Radical Clubs while continuing, not entirely successfully, to try to influence them through the tactic of 'permeation.' The British Marxists on the other hand were doctrinaire schismatics and rejoiced in breaking utterly with the 'bourgeoisie' (who in the course of time proved to be almost everyone). In 1881 the Democratic Federation was launched in pursuit of adult suffrage, the abolition of the House of Lords as a legislative body, and the nationalisation of land. Its leader, H. M. Hyndman, denounced 'the hollowness and hypocrisy of capitalist radicalism' and encouraged the adoption of a collectivist programme. The non-socialists resigned but the Marxist Social Democratic Federation (SDF) which emerged, when compared with the Socialist Party in Germany or the *Parti ouvrier* in France, remained a frustrated and sectarian splinter-group.

The history of modern German socialism dates from May 1863 when Ferdinand Lassalle – 'the only man,' wrote Engels after Lassalle's death in 1864, 'of whom the manufacturers and the swine of the Party of Progress are afraid' – founded the *Allgemeiner Deutscher Arbeitverein*, the German Workers' Association. The tactics employed by Lassalle, who had been imprisoned in 1848 and who was to be prosecuted in later life for inciting the non-possessing classes to hatred and contempt for the possessing classes, were quite straightforward: to wring universal suffrage from the *Junker*-dominated government by pressure and negotiation as the price for a tactical alliance of workers and landowners against the liberal middle class. Marx regarded these tactics and particularly Lassalle's attempt to negotiate directly with Bismarck as a violation of historical science.

At the time when Bismarck was fashioning an Empire and a nation out of the separate German states, any party standing for political popular sovereignty was of the Left. The granting of universal suffrage and of the secret ballot notwithstanding, the Bismarckian system and popular sovereignty were mutually contradictory. A three-class voting system endured in Prussia; no party leader in the Reichstag was granted a place in the ministerial executive; the Reichstag could not initiate laws; revenue was liable to be raised without parliamentary consent; parties could be persecuted or banned at the whim of the Chancellor; and so on.

The non-socialist Left was weak to the point of insignificance. The People's Party, founded in 1865, petty-bourgeois and federalist, was not a force to be reckoned with. The Progressives, who constituted the left wing of the National Liberal Party, were actively

critical of the absence of real democratic control of the executive
and broke with the Liberals completely in 1880. But in Germany
there existed no counterpart to the French Radicals, no powerful
political Left. Leon Trotsky provided a partial explanation when he
wrote of the German bourgeoisie: 'Its consciousness rose against
the objective conditions for its own domination. The revolution
could only be carried out not by it but against it. Democratic institutions represented to its mind not an aim to fight for but a menace
to its welfare.' True as this may be, the fact cannot be ignored that
the French bourgeois Left, for ever grazing on the rich pastures of
its indigenous revolutionary tradition, was a unique phenomenon
both in its size and its achievements. If the political Left was small
in Germany, it was hardly less so in Italy, Spain and Russia. The
British bourgeoisie insisted that the government be accountable to
parliament, but it baulked at the universal suffrage already existing
in Germany. In all these countries, but not in France, the main
burden of the demand for political popular sovereignty was carried
by the economic, or socialist Left in the pre-democratic era. This
divergence certainly presents a dilemma to those who like to isolate
the class factor as the sole determinant of political behaviour and
who dismiss talk of group psychology and national tradition as
idealist abstractions (although it is true that these entities are often
regarded as having descended from Heaven). Engels implicitly
admitted the dilemma when in 1888 he commented on the *Communist Manifesto* of 1848: 'Generally speaking, for the economical
development of the bourgeoisie, England is taken as the typical
country; for its political development, France.' In view of the
Marxist correlation between economic infrastructure and political
superstructure, the question arises – 'typical' of what?

The German Socialist Party (SPD) was founded at Gotha in
1875. Lassallians and Marxists joined forces. The Marxists, whose
formative leaders were Wilhelm Liebknecht and his disciple August
Bebel, were prepared to modify their own Eisenach programme of
1869 in the cause of unity. But reconciliation was not easy. While
Lassalle, like the French socialist Louis Blanc, was convinced that

the existing state could be transformed through universal suffrage into an institution capable of guiding the evolution of socialism, Marx regarded every state-structure as representing the interests of the dominant class. Consequently, socialism would follow only after the proletariat had smashed the bourgeois state. Lassalle, in fact, regarded as feasible for Germany what Marx considered possible for England.

From England, Engels remained in contact with the German socialist leaders until his death in 1895, and his continuing exposition and elaboration of Marxist principles doubtless helped to fortify the SPD in its rejection of the programme of social welfare legislation with which Bismarck hoped to divorce the masses from socialism during the period of the Anti-Socialist Laws (1878–90). In fact the workers did not bite the 'sugared bread', and after 1890 the Party moved from strength to strength on a wave of rapid industrialisation, emerging, in terms of members, candidates elected, organisation and intellectual calibre, as the dominant force in the Second International.

The evidence suggests that the Left is a friend of centralisation and that it fares badly under a federal structure of small states and kingdoms. For forty years Mazzini worked for a unified, democratic and republican Italy, but when in 1870 the work of the Risorgimento was ended, the Italian nation emerged as neither republican nor democratic. In the 1860's Mazzini was committed to a fight on two fronts. On the one hand he attempted to harness the workers' Mutual Aid Societies to the programme of his Action Party, to break down the parochial conservatism that led two-thirds of the delegates to the Florence Congress of 1861 to declare political action to be irrelevant to the workers' interests. On the other, faced with the gradual emergence of socialism, with the conversion of papers like *Il Popolo d'Italia* to the belief that national redemption must find its deeper meaning in a profound social transformation, faced with a new Left which threatened to outflank him while his own mission remained unfulfilled, Mazzini who, with the French radical leader Ledru-Rollin, epitomised the generation of 1848–9 which had been struck down by the Right while hesitating to grasp the hand of the extreme Left, reacted bitterly. He advised the masses 'to preach duty to the classes above you,' and accused the socialists of 'having cancelled man in favour of the sectarian, the free intellect in favour of the formula,' of abandoning moral obligation for the utilitarian happiness principle. In 1866 he founded the Universal Republican Alliance with the purpose of counteracting the propaganda of the IWMA, which he himself had unwittingly joined. Afraid that the bourgeoisie would equate republicanism with the (grossly exaggerated) violence of the Paris Commune (to which so many French Jacobins, the agents of a more advanced tradition, became committed), he denounced the Commune as a denial of God and nationality. In contrast, Garibaldi, the saintly bandit of the early Italian Left, the *conquistador* of the Risorgimento, could feel only compassionate sympathy for the Communards. Uninterested in social cataclysms and economic doctrine, undisturbed by the private ownership of capital, yet dedicated to securing a fair deal for the poor and to uniting the Italian Left, Garibaldi regarded himself as a socialist.

But after 1870 bourgeois and aristocratic Italy, united under conservative auspices, by diplomacy, state power and occasional plebiscites, found room neither for the Mazzinian spirit of democratic regeneration nor for the charitable romanticism of Garibaldi. The so-called constitutional Left which came to power under Depretis in 1876 was not the Left at all. A few radical groups apart, the real Italian Left was henceforth predominantly collectivist; anarchist in the 1870's, reformist in the 1880's (the Italian Workers' Party was founded in 1882, after a small extension of the franchise, and suppressed in 1886 by Depretis), and nominally Marxist after 1892. In that year Mazzinians, Garibaldians, Marxists and disillusioned anarchists came together to form the *Partito socialista italiano* (PSI). United in accepting Marx's analysis of society and its ills, the Party left open the question of his remedies.

The climate of Italian politics in the 1890's, first under the 'left' Premier Crispi, in some senses a precursor of fascism, and after 1896 under di Rudini and Pelloux, was oppressive in the extreme. Crispi made the risings in Sicily, which were an indigenous response to poverty and absentee landlordism, a pretext for the arrest of the socialist leaders. In the North, in Lombardy and Piedmont, the new industrial proletariat stirred restlessly. In 1897 large-scale riots in Milan resulted in the imposition of martial law and the arrest of Filippo Turati and other leaders of the PSI. In such circumstances the Party made what electoral alliances it could with the republicans and radicals, winning thirty-two seats in the elections of June 1900. Crisis bred cohesion. Paradoxically, it was the genuinely liberal Giolitti era, an era of unprecedented Italian prosperity, which inflicted on the PSI a tormented period of recrimination, rift and expulsion.

Russia, 1855–1914

More than thirty years after Pestel's abortive gesture against autocracy, the Russian Left reappeared in the peculiar form of Populism, a movement which had no analogy in western Europe and which was shaped by the unique social structure of Russia, the vast majority of whose population consisted of peasants and whose urban bourgeoisie was hardly less negligible as a force than the proletariat. The Populist, or Narodnik, movement was born in the intellectual ferment following the death of Nicholas I and the defeat in the Crimean War, and culminated in the assassination of Alexander II in 1881, after which it declined and was gradually superseded by Marxism.

Convinced by the events of 1848 that western liberal democracy

№ 4.

Августъ 1902-го г.

ЗАРЯ

СОЦІАЛЬ-ДЕМОКРАТИЧЕСКІЙ
НАУЧНО-ПОЛИТИЧЕСКІЙ ЖУРНАЛЪ

Издается при ближайшемъ участіи

Г. В. ПЛЕХАНОВА, В. И. ЗАСУЛИЧЪ и П. Б. АКСЕЛЬРОДА.

Цѣна 2 руб.

Preis 4 Mark = 5 Francs.

Адресъ для присылки рукописей и денегъ (только изъ заграницы):

J. H. W. Dietz Nachf. (G. m. b. H.) in Stuttgart.

was a sham, Alexander Herzen, the ideological progenitor of Populism, began to convey his theory of peasant socialism in *The Bell*, insisting that the 'mir,' or traditional commune, provided the natural basis for Russian socialism and that the capitalist stage could be by-passed. But if the movement was self-contained, the roots of the doctrine were by no means home-grown. Herzen, Chernyshevsky and the other Narodnik writers avidly absorbed, adapted and synthesised the teachings of the earlier French socialists, particularly Saint-Simon, Fourier and Proudhon. Saint-Simon represented reason, progress, science; Fourier, the small and individualistic unit of socialism; Proudhon stood on his own as the great advocate of the peasant.

Title-page of *Dawn* (*Zarya*), August 1902, showing the names of 65
the early Russian Marxists (all living in exile),
Plekhanov, Vera Zasulich and Axelrod. Later they diverged from Lenin
and lent their support to the Menshevik faction of the Russian Social
Democratic Workers' Party. Under the Tsarist régime,
left-wing journals had a precarious existence.

The most distinguished of the Narodnik theorists was without doubt N. G. Chernyshevsky. Author of the political and didactic novel *What is to be Done?*, a materialist who defended Feuerbach against the claims of Hegelian idealism (Marx had synthesised the two), he saw as the primary task the fostering in the peasantry of a spirit of resistance to authority and of class antagonism. He, like Herzen, believed that Russia could leap the capitalist stage and embark upon industrialisation under socialist auspices. Imprisoned and exiled from 1864 until 1889, he was described by Lenin as 'the only really great Russian writer from the 'fifties until 1888 who was able to keep on the level of an integral philosophical materialism and who spurned the wretched nonsense of the neo-Kantians, positivists, Machians and other muddleheads.'

Whatever their differences in doctrine and strategy, the Populist intelligentsia shared in common a feeling of intense guilt towards the great mass of struggling, superstition-ridden peasants. Anxious to bring education and political enlightenment to the people by way of cheap books and by word of mouth, the alienated students pursued with complete self-sacrifice a dangerous mission, frustrated at every turn by arrests, by peasant inertia and suspicion, by isolation and, although they did not yet appreciate the fact, by the absence of the only class capable of providing sustained and concentrated support, the proletariat.

The growth of Marxism in Russia can be attributed to three factors. First, Populism had patently failed to stimulate anything resembling a revolutionary movement among the peasantry; secondly, Russia experienced rapid industrialisation in the last twenty years of the century, and with it the growth of a proletariat; finally, the rising star of Marxism in the West could not be ignored. In the first instance the classic Marxist progression of feudalism-capitalism-socialism was transposed without modification to the Russian scene by the first Russian Marxist of real distinction, George Plekhanov. The Marxists departed radically from the Populists on the question of the peasant communes which, they believed, could only evolve in the direction of petit-bourgeois capitalism if left to develop according to the logic of their own structure.

As town and country moved apart, Marxism found in an increasingly class-conscious working class its gunpowder. Tsarism inevitably sowed the seeds of its own destruction in attempting to solve its internal contradictions. In order to survive and expand as an imperialist power by modern techniques of warfare it was forced to bring into being the very industrial classes which were bound to destroy it. Strikes became more frequent. In 1893, V. I. Lenin linked up some twenty Marxist groups in the League of Combat, and in 1898 the Russian Social Democratic Workers' Party was founded. In 1901, after the period in Siberia which had become the routine apprenticeship (or graveyard) of the Russian revolutionist, Lenin began to make heard his authoritative voice in *The Spark* and *The Dawn*.

Lenin had been briefly a landlord at Alakaeva. He knew the peasantry, their mentality and their aspirations. Far from comprising, as the Populists had tended to assume, a homogeneous class, they were, he realised, an estate subdivided into classes. Politically, their diverse relationships to agricultural capital and to landownership would count for more than their common connection to the agricultural form of production. Lenin's basic hypothesis was that in Russia the nascent proletariat could harness the whole peasantry to the overthrow of the autocracy by appealing to their landhunger. This would complete the 'bourgeois democratic' revolution. The richer peasants, or kulaks, would benefit most from the distribution of the large estates (as in fact proved to be the case in 1917–18) and so cease to be an objectively revolutionary force. The workers, acting in concert with the poor or landless peasants, would then carry the revolution a stage further and proceed to collectivisation. In the meantime, in order to rouse the working class to its historical mission, a dedicated élite of revolutionaries, trained in Marxism and trained also in the clandestine techniques necessitated by a police state, must propagate a proper class consciousness, combatting the deviationist tendencies towards 'negative' trade unionism, reformism, localism and so forth. Unlike the syndicalists in France, Lenin had no faith in proletarian spontaneity. 'Class political consciousness,' he wrote, 'can be brought to the workers only *from without*, that is, only from outside the economic struggle, from outside the sphere of relations between employers and workers.'

Before 1900 there was no exclusively political Left in Russia. The democrats were also socialists. But at the turn of the century the urban bourgeoisie began to warm towards western liberalism and radicalism. In 1904, as unrest gathered with the Russo–Japanese war, the leader of the Constitutional Democrats (Cadets), Paul Miliukov, conferred with Struve, Chernov and other leaders of the Socialist Revolutionary Party, a loosely organised body born from the collaboration of scattered Narodnik groups and inheriting from the 1870's the demand for democratic, socialist and decentralised peasant government. The conference issued an appeal for universal suffrage and the basic freedoms. The Cadets, whose attitude bore resemblances to that of French radicalism and also to Giolittian liberalism, represented the moderate Left under the consistently undemocratic régime which endured in Russia until 1917. Miliukov became the foremost opposition leader in the Duma.

The inter-war years

The First World War proved the ruin of the Second International. The anti-patriotic slogans and the endless debates in socialist and syndicalist circles about an international general strike in the event of war were mocked in August 1914 by the steady tramp of boots and by the fervour of patriotism which swept the workers and, with a few exceptions, their leaders as well. From Switzerland in 1915 Lenin launched the Zimmerwald movement, urging the transformation of the imperialist war into an international civil war. The physical cost of the war, in terms of death, suffering and mutilation, grew progressively more terrible, breeding a new spirit of revolt in the trenches and factories. By October 1917, when the

Bolshevik revolution added new authority to Leninism, the old leaders of the Second International had come to be regarded as traitors by a large minority of the socialist movement. What followed was the most profound and systematic schism in the history of the Left. In February 1919 the Second International met at Berne and roundly condemned Bolshevism. A month later, the Third International (Comintern) was launched in Moscow, attracting to itself the left-wing of almost every Socialist Party in Europe. A wave of revolutionary violence struck Germany, Hungary, Italy and France in rapid succession.

By the end of 1920 the tide had receded. Russia alone remained a communist state, isolated, feared and unrecognised by the nations of the world. Western views of the Bolshevik reality were distorted either by idealisation or, more commonly, fear, and always by ignorance. The bourgeoisie trembled as once it had trembled before the Jacobins. Its press portrayed Lenin and Trotsky as super-human devils incarnating a primitive, destructive and inhuman barbarism. Capitalism achieved a temporary stability and the Communist Parties found themselves engaged in a defensive battle against fascism and right-wing authoritarianism in general. In France and Spain the Left was eventually overwhelmed by superior force; in Italy and Germany it went under with hardly a fight.

The responsibility for the advent to power of Mussolini in 1922 and Hitler in 1933 cannot, of course, be laid at the door of socialists and communists alone. More important because more decisive were the anti-socialist prejudices of Giolitti, Nitti and the Italian Liberal leaders on the one hand, and of Hugenberg, Hindenberg, von Papen, von Schleicher and the German right-wing politicians on the other. Fascinated by the vision of fascism as a useful bludgeon with which to hammer the Reds, they blundered in dismissing it as a purely negative force which would shed its dynamic appeal once in power.

Nevertheless, on both occasions the Left was guilty of fatal miscalculations. The Italian communists, who had recently severed their connections with the Socialist Party, refused to consider, despite the warnings of the Turin leader Antonio Gramsci, the formation of an anti-fascist united front. Bordiga and the 'ultras' prevailed in their view that a fascist *coup* would carry no more disastrous consequences than would a routine change of cabinet. On 29 October 1922, a Party paper declared: 'In the present conflict . . . (the workers) cannot side with the so-called constitutional government . . .'. Within twenty-four hours the paper had been liquidated.

Ten years later the same pattern repeated itself in Germany with appalling precision. The German communists had evidently learned nothing either from the Italian precedent or from the turbulent, *coup*-ridden history of the Weimar Republic. Regardless of the ominous growth of the Nazis at a time of chronic unemployment, the German Communist Party, now a force to be reckoned with and represented by almost 100 deputies in the Reichstag, observed a ritualistic obedience to the current Comintern line and persisted in branding the socialists 'social-fascists.' The communists associated themselves, moreover, with the Nazi-inspired campaign which resulted in the overthrow in 1932 of the socialist regional government in Prussia. Any political upheaval, by whatever source it was inspired, would ultimately benefit the working class; revolution would follow close on the heels of the counter-revolution. Or so the current Stalinist orthodoxy insisted.

In 1934, a year after the German communists had learned their lesson, the Bulgarian Party submitted to a military *coup* while busily absorbed in a struggle against the Peasants' Union. It was not until 1935 that Dimitrov officially recognised these errors on behalf of the Comintern (without, however, attributing them to the Comintern and still less to their ultimate source, Stalin) and gave his blessing to the popular front tactics which were soon to be employed in France and Spain.

If the communists consistently fell into the same trap – dogmatic sectarianism – the errors of the Italian socialists and of their German colleagues little resembled one another. The majority of the Italian Socialist Party was itself sectarian, revolutionary and

anxious to join the Comintern. When the leader of the reformist wing, Turati, tried in desperation to form an anti-fascist coalition government, the Party disowned him and proceeded to expel the reformists at the very moment of the fascist March on Rome. The Germans on the other hand, while far more aware of the dangers, showed themselves incapable of resolute action, of employing their own para-military organisation, the *Reichsbanner*, to meet force with force. They offered no resistance when von Papen ejected the socialist government of Prussia. Sectarian though the communists were, the socialists were less than enthusiastic about forming a working partnership. Only in Spain and Austria did socialism go down fighting. When the conservative Chancellor Dollfuss arrested their leaders, the workers of Linz and Vienna rose and fought bravely until they were bombarded into submission.

The Left paid heavily for its mistakes. The Italian socialist leaders Modigliani, Treves, Turati and Nenni were able to leave the country, but others were less fortunate. Matteoti was murdered. In March 1923, 10,000 communists were arrested. The brilliant and humane Gramsci died in a prison. So also did Thaelmann, the leader of the German communists. The eighty-one communist deputies elected in March 1933 went not to the Reichstag but to concentration camps.

Left: Mussolini takes power, 1922. The future dictator, and former socialist, entering the Quirinal to be received by King Victor Emmanuel, after the fascist 'March on Rome'. Within four years Mussolini had crushed all political opposition; not for the last time in this century, the Left paid dearly for its divisions.

Right: Pietro Nenni, grand old man of Italian socialism, and the last of the European socialist leaders to remain faithful to Marxism and to retain a guarded friendship for the communists. When Nenni entered a Centre-Left government coalition in 1963, both these attitudes were put in doubt.

Since the Second World War

Despite the temporary unity of purpose and action achieved by the European Left after the Nazi attack on the USSR in 1941, and despite the universal hopes for the creation of a regenerated, socialised society after the war, the onset of the Cold War and of the division of the world into two antagnostic camps revived and even accentuated the old divisions. In 1945 Léon Blum persuaded the Socialist Party to reject the communist offer of a united French workers' party. Nevertheless, socialists and communists were agreed in calling for the abolition of the Third Republic and for the institution of a Constituent Assembly with sovereign powers. The nation refused to make the Assembly sovereign but elected 302 socialist and communist deputies out of a total of 586, the first and last time that the Left, the real as opposed to the nominal Left, had an absolute majority. But the unrestricted power enjoyed at this time by the Labour Party in Britain eluded it. In 1947 the communists left the government and went into permanent opposition, while the socialists accepted the Atlantic Alliance and began to assume a role analogous to that of the Radicals under the later Third Republic. The Left grew smaller. The Catholic MRP shed its 'Bevanite' faction and moved to the Centre-Right. Small Marxist or neo-Marxist groups rebelling against the necessity of choice between two great world powers sprang into being only to be crushed by that very necessity. The *Parti socialiste unitaire* and the *Rassemblement Démocratique Révolutionnaire* (the creation of J.-P. Sartre and Albert Camus) were the most notable, but they made no impression on the electorate. Yet independent Marxism showed a remarkable capacity to survive and even flourish in the face of Stalinism. The *Parti Socialiste Autonome*, to which Mendès-France became committed after his break with the Radicals, and its successor the *Parti Socialiste Unifié*, adopted a programme of socialism, eventual workers' control of industry, and democratic – as opposed to technocratic – planning. The Hungarian revolution, which cost the French and British (particularly the British) Communist Parties much of their support among intellectuals, paradoxically heralded in both countries a renaissance of Marxist studies in the fields of philosophy, sociology, economics and literature.

From 1934 onward the Italian socialist leader Pietro Nenni had collaborated closely with the communists in exile. After the war Nenni became the guiding spirit in inducing his Party to sign a unity-of-action pact with the communists. In some towns such as Rome the two Parties acted as a single, cohesive entity. Against this the socialist right-wing rebelled and in 1947 Saragat formed the Italian Workers' Party to which some fifty of the 115 PSI deputies adhered. Further splits, compromises and reconciliations among those opposed to the Nenni policy culminated in 1951 in the foundation of the Italian Social Democratic Party which supported the Atlantic Alliance and which, in 1953, became part of a Centre electoral coalition embracing the republicans and liberals. Of all the European socialist leaders, Nenni was certainly the one closest in sympathy with the communists, but after eighteen years of intransigent opposition the offer in 1963 to participate in a new Centre-Left government was one that Nenni felt unable to resist. But the price – acceptance of the Atlantic Alliance and a compromise on domestic issues with the Christian Democrats – was held by many in the Party to be too dear.

5 Revolution or reform ? 1

Western Europe, 1789–1840's

Neither philosophically nor historically do revolution and reform constitute a simple dichotomy. Nevertheless the history of the European Left reveals a fundamental divergence between those who have committed themselves to a progressive evolution and those who have worked for a violent showdown, between those confident in the power of moral persuasion and those who regard force as the indispensable midwife of social regeneration.

Reformism, wrote Trotsky, 'is the product of theoretical limitations, a short memory, or just simply hypocrisy.' But in fact the reformist is likely to be separated from the revolutionary by three principal factors, doctrinal, circumstantial and temperamental: in other words, the militant may resort to revolutionary violence because he has read and absorbed Marx or Bakunin; or because his political opponents are themselves either violent or intransigent; or because he is 'by nature' a violent man. In the formation of revolutionary groups all three factors normally operate, although in varying proportions. Of the three, the last is by far the most difficult to detect and define.

The Babouvists – the communist conspirators led by Gracchus Babeuf in 1796 – derived their revolutionary theory partly from the Jacobins and partly from the force of circumstances. So long as the revolution had progressed, Babeuf had been prepared to observe and to approve, but the reaction of Thermidor 1794, which suppressed Jacobinism in the interests of the purely bourgeois revolution and which a year later imposed a high tax qualification on voters, bred among left-wing democrats an increasing despair. Babeuf protested against the new constitution and was imprisoned. He and his friends then resorted to conspiracy and developed a theory of the necessity of a well-planned *coup* in a thoroughly indoctrinated area, preferably Paris. The plot was discovered and Babeuf executed.

The thirty years which followed the Treaty of Vienna of 1815, the high period of the Holy Alliance and of monarchical reaction,

marked the nadir of the Left, withering its ranks and compressing its energies into small secret societies which no longer regarded the people as revolutionary material. In August 1820, 600 students of *Les Amis de la Vérité* armed themselves and prepared to overthrow the Bourbon monarchy. They failed. One abortive *coup* followed another.

Tory Britain, the banker and navy of the European counter-revolution, its domestic reflexes instinctively repressive, financially visionary and economically blind, was also not without its trouble-makers. The old Jacobinism flared up for the last time in Despard's conspiracy in 1802, and there is evidence to link the 'underground' of that year with that of 1812. British violence was more firmly rooted in the nascent working class than was the case in France or elsewhere; in 1812 more troops were deployed in the disturbed areas than Wellington had in the Peninsula. The Luddites – the machine-breakers – often regarded as not only economically re-trograde but also completely non-political, were in fact highly organised in Nottinghamshire and Yorkshire, and their resent-ments were liable to be channelled into revolutionary paths by democrat and Paineite agitators. Under the rigidly conservative Liverpool government the socialist followers of Thomas Spence and some of the Hampden Clubs fostered a climate of violence which culminated in the Cato Street Conspiracy to assassinate the entire cabinet.

Chartist demonstration on Kennington Common, 1848. 75
Chartism, although internally divided between socialists and
non-socialists, proponents of physical force and proponents
of moral force, broadly unified the British democratic Left from
1837 until 1848. After its collapse in that year, the
Left did not properly revive until the 1880's.

In France, the advent of the July monarchy in 1830 had the
initial effect of reviving democratic republicanism among sections
of the middle class and of encouraging the growth of a moderate,
reformist Left. Armand Carrel, editor of *Le National*, advised
against all violence, while Etienne Cabet, who travelled from
democracy to communism and whose paper, *Populaire*, was read
by the Parisian workers, also pointed to the self-defeating aspects of
violence. The Committee of the *Société des Droits de l'Homme* was
divided between 'legal pacifists' such as Raspail and those, like
Lesbon, whose thoughts were never far removed from the barricades. The action of the government in 1834, when 164 republican
leaders, headed by Cavaignac, were put on trial as the result of an
uprising at Lyons, inevitably played into the hands of the revolutionaries. In May 1839 Blanqui and Barbès attempted to seize
power in Paris.

The thought of Auguste Blanqui, who had learnt his revolutionary communism largely from Buonarroti, a survivor of the
Babouvist conspiracy, and who can be regarded as the outstanding
French revolutionary leader in the nineteenth century, was extre-
mely unco-ordinated. Throughout his life a practitioner of the élitist
coup, of the seizure of power by a dedicated band of revolutionaries,
he was, paradoxically, emphatic that history would *inevitably* wit-
ness the triumph of 'association' over egotistical individualism.
Unlike Marx, he asserted the primacy of pure politics; all the
necessary social changes would follow the seizure of power. Consequently he was little interested in carrying his ideology to the
trade unions and the labour movement in general, and his attention
was focused, in the Jacobin tradition, on the metropolis rather
than the industrial areas: unlike Marx, he did not regard the proletariat as being destined or able to bring about its own liberation.

But a single environment need not breed a single response. Just
as Marx was challenged by Lassalle in the 1860's, so Louis Blanc's
belief, similar to Lassalle's, that capitalism could be transformed
into socialism through the agency of universal suffrage and progressive reform, seriously rivalled Blanqui's revolutionary doctrine

Auguste Blanqui, French revolutionary, and direct heir to the tradition of Babeuf and Buonarroti. An advocate of a violent *coup*, proletarian dictatorship and communism, Blanqui did not appreciate the need to root his party in the proletarian masses of the new industrial complexes. His long life (1805–81) was a saga of failure, imprisonment and unflagging idealism. *Below*: First victim of the Revolution of July 1830 taken to the Place des Victoires, Paris. The traditions of the Great Revolution were remembered.

in the 1840's. In the first weeks of democratic harmony which followed the revolution of February 1848 Blanc seemed vindicated, but as the bourgeois Republic sought to stabilise itself and to frustrate any socialist movement, evolutionary or otherwise, Blanqui's *Société Républicaine Centrale* and Barbès' *Club de la Révolution* began to attract wider support.

The British Left has always been a reluctant revolutionary. The

Chartists were divided, partly by temperament and doctrine, but more obviously between skilled workers and craftsmen on the one hand and the unskilled proletariat on the other, between the advocates of 'physical force' and 'moral force.' O'Brien and George Julian Harney, both well versed in Jacobinism, were closest in spirit to Blanqui and the French extremists. The demagogic O'Connor, whose influence lay primarily in the industrial North, was more inclined to violence than Lovett, who spoke for the better educated workers and artisans in the London area and whose twin moral idols were education and persuasion. In 1839 the moderates began to withdraw from the Chartist General Convention when it adopted a resolution supporting the right of the people to arm.

In the period before 1848, British left-wing violence was inclined to differ from the French on two main counts. First, it was more pragmatic and less doctrinaire, less assured theoretically that democracy or socialism can be achieved only by revolution, and more inclined to warn 'if they won't give way, we'll fight.' This divergence partially accounts for the persistence of a revolutionary tradition in France and for its episodic character in Britain. Secondly, and relatedly, British violence tended to originate in the factory areas, among the workers themselves, rather than among intellectuals in the capital. It was more spontaneous and less calculated.

Once it had become clear that neither a Liberal nor a Tory government would give way to their democratic demands, the Chartist workers began to arm and drill in Lancashire, Wales and elsewhere. Martial law was declared in Birmingham. An insurrectionary leaflet of 1839 urged: 'when you strike . . . let the blood of all you suspect moisten the soil of your native land that you may for ever destroy even the remembrance of your poverty and shame.' In November a small insurrection occurred at Newport, with ten killed and fifty wounded. Between April 1839 and June 1840, the government responded to the wave of violence by deploying troops and by the arrest of 442 Chartist leaders in England and Wales. Devoid of united and purposeful leadership, the workers began to retreat. A Blanqui might be prepared to spend half his life in jail, but the worker's freedom to revolt is limited by the necessity of economic survival, by the slender margin which stands between his family and starvation. Weakened by the apparent antithesis between the worker's livelihood and his political aspirations, and by the forceful self-confidence of the propertied classes, revolutionary Chartism had to admit defeat.

Western Europe, 1840's—1914

In German communism, which turned decisively from the utopian to the revolutionary road in the 1840's, is to be found the bridge between the extreme Left of the early nineteenth century and that of the late, between a socialism as yet divorced from the working class and a socialism rooted in the masses. The German exiles were revolutionaries – and hence exiles. Weitling, inspired by Blanqui, thought in terms of *coups*, while Karl Schapper and Joseph Moll expressed the dominant feeling within the Federation of the Just in calling for an immediate proletarian seizure of power. In contrast, Marx was inclined to the view that the first step in Germany must consist of a bourgeois revolution on the lines of 1789. When in 1848 the left-wing element of the Rhineland middle class invited him to edit the *Neue Rheinische Zeitung* he accepted, simultaneously urging through its pages the bourgeoisie to construct a united German nation out of the wreckage of feudalism, and the proletariat to support them. The *Communist Manifesto* in fact allows of two diverse interpretations of the probable tempo of the revolution. It explains the evolutionary process by which capitalism progressively pauperises the majority of the population, swelling the ranks of the proletariat and leading ultimately to the socialist revolution. But elsewhere one reads: 'the bourgeois revolution in Germany will be but the prelude to an immediately following proletarian revolution.' Marx, passionately committed to the fulfilment of his prophecy in his own country, and implicitly invoking what Trotsky was later to call 'permanent revolution,' argued that the German workers were more advanced than the English or French had been at the time of their bourgeois revolutions and would on this account be able to 'jump the gun'. But it was Marx who had jumped the gun.

Taken in its totality and full reflectiveness, Marx's work suggests five necessary conditions for revolution: the bourgeoisie in power; the disappearance of intermediary classes; the proletariat is the immense majority; the workers are concerted and organised; they are unable to defend their standard of living. Before 1848 only the last of these factors was operative. The universal collapse of the revolutions of 1848 and the period of prosperous stability which followed led Marx to concede in 1866 that certain countries, such as Britain and America, might pass to socialism by peaceful means. But, he continued to insist, 'in the majority of the continental countries forcible means must be used as the crow-bar of our revolution . . .' Marx had begun to fit spare, empirical parts to an essentially anti-empirical machine – historical materialism.

For the benefit of the later German socialists, Engels continued to emphasise the political indispensability of force and spoke of 'the immense moral and spiritual impetus which has resulted from every victorious revolution', arguing that a violent collision in Germany would wipe out the servility which had permeated the national consciousness since the Thirty Years War. Embarrassed, the SPD put out a bowdlerised version of his introduction to Marx's *The Class Struggles in France*, a version which gave the impression that he was opposed to all violence. The Erfurt Programme of 1891 made no reference to violent revolution, despite the twelve years of repression from which the Party had just emerged.

The German Party, in fact, was deeply divided, and it was at this period that there developed within its ranks the most articulate of controversies concerning the revolution-reform dichotomy. In 1891 the Munich deputy Vollmar sang the praises of 'slow, organic evolution.' Eduard Bernstein, who was to become the leading theoretician of 'revisionism' (i.e. of a revision of Marxism), had, while exiled in Britain, begun to absorb and accept the gradualism of Fabians like Hubert Bland, at the same time developing a comprehensive critique of Marx's basic hypotheses. In 1899 he published the 'Bible' of revisionism, *The Suppositions of Socialism and the Problems of Social Democracy*. Writing after nearly twenty years of almost uninterrupted prosperity, he challenged Marx's prediction of the increasing pauperisation of all but the largest capitalists. Instead of an ever-sharpening clash of opposing forces, the intensification of social contradictions, he discerned a process of evolutionary reconciliation based on *diminishing* class antagonisms. It followed that if socialism could not be guaranteed as the inevitable outcome of quasi-mechanical historical forces, it must be a matter of personal, moral choice. Moreover, the action following such a choice would have to align itself with the movement of society, that is to say it would have to be gradualist, conciliatory and indeed empirical.

The underlying environmental factor which generated this schism within German socialism lay in differences of regional economic development and of political structure. In the areas of heavy industry such as the Rhur, Silesia and Saxony the trend was generally in accordance with Marx's prediction that expanding monopolies would swallow smaller businesses. In Prussia, where a three-class voting system was in force, there existed a large class of landless agricultural labourers. But in the South and West the small farmers and businesses were prospering and it was among southern socialists like Vollmar, David, Frank and Eisner that revisionism made most headway. From this quarter, and from Bernstein, came the plea that the Party should promise assistance to the land-owning peasantry and so win over their often decisive vote, whereas Kautsky and the orthodox Marxists opposed any financial concessions which would bolster the peasant against large-scale capitalist farming and so frustrate the iron laws of history.

In the event, the Party tended to remain revolutionary in theory (Bernstein narrowly escaped expulsion) while becoming increasingly reformist in practice. Despite the wave of revolutionary enthusiasm which swept the SPD at the time of the 1905 revolution in

Russia, those who could be identified as consistently intransigent Marxists formed an increasingly small, isolated and vociferous left wing, Rosa Luxemburg, Karl Liebknecht, Franz Mehring and Konrad Haenisch being among the most notable. In her *Reform or Revolution* (1888), Rosa Luxemburg argued that modern industrial society could be transformed only by revolution and that legislation, constitutions and codified rights were but the 'vegetative stage of society.' Arrested in Warsaw in 1906 and deported to Germany, she wrote *The Mass Strike, the Party and the Labour Unions*, a document strongly urging revolutionary action based on the general strike. Regarding reforms as valuable only in so far as they provided a method of rehearsal, of training the proletariat for cohesive action, she strongly criticised Bernstein and Jaurès. By 1914 there was no disguising the preponderantly reformist character of the Party leadership.

In France, the struggle between the exponents of revolution and reform initially took place not within a single party but on the basis of rival socialist groups. Jules Guesde, at one time an anarchist, founded in 1879 the Marxist *Parti ouvrier* and was at once challenged by Paul Brousse's 'Possibilists.' Guesdism gained ground in the minefields of the Nord and the Pas de Calais while the Possibilists found more support in Paris, the Loire and areas where class struggle was less acute. Guesde's colleague and theoretician Paul Lafargue perhaps echoed his father-in-law Marx's own vision when he described the future revolution in France as gathering impetus in the industrial towns, incorporating the local peasants, challenging the bourgeois-dominated sea ports, imprisoning the capitalist leaders and creating a central state power based on the support of the revolutionary masses. Guesde, whom Marx and Engels regarded as unduly doctrinaire, impatient and schematic, tended, in view of the strength of the political Left in France, to dismiss anti-clericalism and anti-militarism as purely bourgeois problems. He refused to choose between the neo-Bonapartist General Boulanger and his republican opponents in the crisis of 1887–9.

Right: Rosa Luxemburg, a leader of the left wing of German Social Democracy, with Lili Braun (on the left) in 1906.
Below: Eduard Bernstein, pioneer of the theoretical revision of Marxist doctrine and advocate of evolutionary socialism.

After 1883 there existed four socialist organisations in France competing for the workers' allegiance, two reformist (Broussists and Allemanists) and two revolutionary (Guesdists and Blanquists). As a Marxist, Guesde rejected as futile both anarchist violence and the Blanquist tradition of *coups*. In theory, he like Marx appreciated the importance of winning over the labour movement and of carrying on the work of the First International. But in practice Marxism made little headway within the trade unions before 1914.

It was in the 1890's that Jean Jaurès, the greatest and best-loved of French socialist leaders, appeared as a force on the political scene. A former radical and a brilliant scholar, Jaurès was a reformist idealist in the sense of hoping that the moral advancement of the middle class might forestall total class war. Unlike Guesde he came to see in the Dreyfus affair and in the concomitant threat to the Republic an issue on which the proletariat must make its voice heard; unlike the extreme insurrectionist Gustave Hervé, he held that resort to the general strike should be confined only to the most

Below left: Jean Jaurès, leader of the French Socialist Party in the Chamber of Deputies until his assassination in 1914. A tribune of the people and a scholar, he was deeply opposed to violence. But he remained immune to the siren call of the more flexible and astute bourgeois politicians who made periodic advances towards the reformist socialists. The Italian Liberal Premier Giovanni Giolitti (*below right*) made full use of this intelligent strategy.

desperate situations; unlike both, he regarded universal suffrage as the legitimate 'revolutionary' weapon of the masses. But Jaurès never travelled as far along the reformist road as did Briand, Viviani and Alexandre Millerand, who in 1903 published his *Le Socialisme reformiste français*, in which he suggested that the workers come to terms with their employers and that private property be not so much abolished as extended to all.

It was apparently Guesde who triumphed when, following the Amsterdam Congress of the Second International in 1904, the two main French socialist factions joined forces with the declaration that the new Party, the *Section Française de l'Internationale Ouvrière* (SFIO), was revolutionary and not reformist. But it was Jaurès who, as the leading socialist tribune in the Chamber of Deputies and as editor of *l'Humanité*, was to exercise the dominant influence in the years before his assassination in 1914.

In Italy, the latent rift between revolutionaries and reformists within the PSI did not come to the surface until after 1900, when a

decade of blind reaction gave way to an era of genuinely liberal advance. In Giolitti the Party had to face a courtier of the workers more enlightened than Bismarck and more subtle than Clemenceau or Lloyd George. Tolerant towards strikes, critical of bourgeois egoism, the initiator of insurance schemes, factory legislation, subsidies to co-operatives and, in 1911, of manhood suffrage, Giolitti and his policy favoured the reformist wing of the PSI led by Turati and reduced the appeal of Lazzari and the Marxists. In 1908 the revolutionary syndicalists rebelled against this swing to the right and withdrew from the Party. A single event swung the pendulum back – the Libyan war in 1911. The ultra-reformists, headed by Bissolati and Bonomi, argued that a single colonialist adventure did not outweigh Giolitti's innumerable achievements, but an angry left wing eloquently represented by the young orator Mussolini forced their explusion in 1912. Italian socialism girded its loins for 'red week' in 1914 and for the quasi-revolutionary movements of 1918–20.

It will take a work of genius to analyse the intricate complex of social inhibitions, safety-valves, recreational outlets, economic relationships, snobberies and periods of enlightened government which made of the British worker a reformist and enabled him to channel his frustrations into nonconformist chapels, football matches, pubs and patriotic songs. The Fabians, whose journal, *The Practical Socialist*, subtitled itself in January 1887, 'a monthly review of evolutionary or non-revolutionary socialism,' told him that landlords and capitalists would gradually see the light and so accept the demands of justice without too bitter a struggle. The Labour Party informed him that revolutions and revolutionary theory were the mark of the backwardness of the savages who inhabited the continent of Europe. On rare occasions the British worker was inclined to think again, as was the case during the years immediately preceding the First World War, when immense fortunes were being amassed, when the organic connection between the unions and the Party was being challenged by the Right, when troops were being sent to the mining areas and when the majority of Labour MP's elected in or after 1906 – the independent socialist Victor Grayson was a notable exception – had evidently either gone to sleep or sold out to the system. In 1908 Ben Tillett published a book in which he called the Labour MP's 'sheer hypocrites' who had repaid 'with gross betrayal the class that willingly supports them.' Tillett turned not to Marxism but to another continental product – revolutionary syndicalism. As in 1832–4, so also in 1910–13 a section of the militant proletariat lost faith in the reforming state and attempted to impose its will by violent economic action.

Closely related to the reformist current was another issue, another 'ism' which confronted all the member parties of the Second International on a theoretical level and those working in bourgeois-democratic states on a practical level. The word 'participationism' covered the problem as to whether a socialist could in any circumstances legitimately accept a post or ministry in a non-socialist government. The question first arose as a consequence of the Dreyfus affair and of Waldeck-Rousseau's attempt to rally all left-wing forces in defence of the democratic Republic. In 1899 Millerand joined the government with the approval of Jaurès but in the teeth of Guesde's scornful hostility. 'If we support a Ministry,' explained Jaurès, 'it is not for the sake of supporting it, but in order to prevent the more evil Ministries that might do us harm.' Guesde retorted that Millerand had by his action obliged himself to support the government's military budget and with it the whole mechanism of imperialism (the French communists were to face a similar complication in the period 1945–7). A Congress of all socialist groups in December 1899 endorsed Guesde's point of view and in the following year 'participationism' was condemned by the International, the Germans (who were never invited to join a government but who made periodic electoral alliances with the Centre Party and supported the more progressive governments in the provincial *Lander*) wholeheartedly supporting Guesde against Jaurès.

This decision was bound to have a bearing on Italian politics in the Giolitti era. In 1903 Turati was invited to join the government and would have done so had not the PSI, mindful of the International's attitude and suspicious of any compromise with capitalist society, prevented him. Some years later the invitation was extended to Bissolati, but the Party remained resolute. The suspicions of the 'doctrinaires' were not in fact without foundation. Of those who supported Millerand's action, Millerand himself, Briand and Viviani soon became the avowed enemies of socialism. Bissolati was expelled from the PSI in 1912. The bourgeois-democratic state offered the socialist politician a permanent prospect of lucrative seduction; once ambushed, he would not be long in jettisoning his ideals. Ultimately, however, it was not the prospect of personal advancement but patriotism which broke down all inhibitions and which led even Guesde to join the government in 1914. Paradoxically Guesde, who had singled out the act of implicitly supporting the military budget as the most heinous betrayal of socialist principles in 1899, insisted initially in 1914 that in joining the government the one aspect of its policy which socialists would unquestioningly uphold was the war effort!

Russia, 1855–1914

Further afield in Russia the debate took an altogether different form. In the Populist era there was no Marxist orthodoxy to revise, no government offering participation and little hope of real reform. Consequently the Populists, like the Russian Marxists after them, argued about revolutionary methods and tempo, dividing broadly between those who favoured immediate acts of violence and those who pinned their hopes on the progressive education and indoctrination of the peasant masses. After the liberation of the serfs in 1861, Herzen parted from his followers on the question of violence. The anarchist strategy, of which the arch-apostle was Bakunin, relied on terror and assassination, expecting the state to collapse once its jugular vein had been severed. The ruthless nihilist Nechaev, whose ill-fated activities inspired Dostoevsky's novel *The Possessed*, was the most extreme exponent of this philosophy. In

Bakunin, a Russian aristocrat who became the apostle of violent revolution. He looked forward to an anarchist society delivered from the oppressive institutions of government, and collectivist in economic structure. Much misunderstood, Bakunin was in reality neither a nihilist nor a demon. Unfortunately, most of the *coups* with which he was associated between 1848 and 1876 failed to rise above the level of comic opera.

contrast, the 'Go to the People' movement led by Natanson and Chaikovsky and supported by the socialist writer Pierre Lavrov rejected cataclysmic violence and Machiavellian plots in favour of an open, educational mission to the peasants. But the arrest of 770 such missionaries swung the pendulum once more towards physical force. The last of the major Populist revolutionary movements, Land and Liberty, split in 1878 between the Black Earth Distribution, the propagandists and preachers, and The People's Will, a network of terrorist groups headed by Andrei Zhelyabov. There were clashes in St. Petersburg; the Governors of St Petersburg and Kharkov were shot; and in 1881 Alexander II was assassinated. But no amount of bravery and self-sacrifice can atone for the absence of an industrial revolution. Tsars and Governors were expendable, reproductive and prepared to carry repression to its logical conclusion. Absolute, unfaltering repression is always effective.

The issue which divided the Russian Social Democrats was not so much 'revolution or reform?' as 'revolution sooner or later?' The Bolshevik–Leninist analysis of the potential sources and inter-relationships of the revolutionary strata suggested the need for constant vigilance, for revolutionary opportunism. The Mensheviks, led by Martov and Dan and guided by Plekhanov and Axelrod, were unwilling to adapt the classic Marxist progression to Russian conditions and insisted that socialism could only follow a fully developed stage of bourgeois democracy based on a properly capitalist economy. For Lenin, revolution was action, not evolution. In fact, justifications for both the Bolshevik and Menshevik attitudes are to be found side-by-side in the *Communist Manifesto*. Although the general pattern of historical materialism lays emphasis on the *evolutionary* development of economic forces, Marx, when faced with an actual political crisis, almost invariably became excited by the prospect of an imminent proletarian revolution.

The revolution of 1905 confirmed both groups in their conviction of the correctness of their position. The Mensheviks pointed to the proven unreliability of the peasants and Lenin to the weakness of the Russian bourgeoisie in the face of the autocracy. Between the two factions and on his own ground stood Trotsky. According to his theory of 'permanent revolution' – a theory for which many precedents are to be found in the works of Marx and Engels – a continuous process had to be set in motion, first achieving the 'democratic' revolution, then moving towards socialism, and finally galvanising the internal mechanism of the socialist revolution itself. Ultimately, the Russian workers would depend on the support of the foreign proletariat. (Lenin was inclined to agree that the Russian revolution could not long survive in isolation.) Thus the permanent revolution would connect the liquidation of medievalism with socialism through a series of sharpening social clashes. Trotsky did not believe that the peasantry could ever play an independent political role; history showed that they must be taken by the collar, either by the bourgeoisie or by the workers. The workers could maintain their temporary initiative only by carrying the class struggle into the villages and by enforcing rapid collectivisation. 'In no way must it be supposed that a proletarian government, on expropriating the privately-owned estates carrying on production on a large scale, would break these up and sell them for exploitation to small producers.' It was on this point, and particularly on the issue of tempo, that Lenin and Trotsky diverged most sharply.

6 Revolution or reform? 2

The revolutionary wave, 1918–1921

The issue of revolution or reform was revived soon after the outbreak of the First World War by Lenin's Zimmerwald movement.
Two main factions soon emerged: a majority, calling for an immediate peace, and a Leninist minority, urging the transformation
of the 'imperialist' war into an international civil war. The Bolshevik revolution, which immeasurably strengthened the prestige
of the Leninists, made for thousands a sacred text of Lenin's *The
State and Revolution* in which he wrote: 'the replacement of the
bourgeois by the proletarian state is impossible without a violent
revolution.' He scathingly denounced as 'social patriots' and as
lackeys of the bourgeoisie Scheidemann, Ebert, Legien and David
in Germany, the majority of the French Socialist Party, the Belgian
Vandervelde, Turati and Treves in Italy; he had nothing but contempt for the equivocating 'Centre' represented by Kautsky and by
Longuet in France. Trotsky produced a rousing Manifesto for the
First Congress of the Communist International in March 1919, a
call to universal revolution framed within the stark alternative –
seize power or perish.

Nevertheless, the influence of Moscow on the European upheavals of 1918–20 was more indirect than direct, more a matter of
inspiration than of direct organisation. Cut off by the civil war and
by the Allied blockade, the Bolsheviks lacked even reliable information. In a telegram to the Hungarian communist Bela Kun, dated
23 March 1919, Lenin asked: 'have the communists a majority in
the government? When will the congress of soviets take place?
What does the socialist recognition of the dictatorship of the proletariat really amount to?' In a message of greetings to the Bavarian
Soviet Republic, dated 27 April 1919, he appealed: 'we request
insistently that you give us more frequent and concrete information
...' Four months later, he complained in a message to the Italian
Marxists Serrati and Lazzari: 'we know very little about your
movement; we have no documents whatever.'

Despite Trotsky's Manifesto, neither the Comintern nor the

The German revolution, 1918–19. A leader of the right wing of the
SPD, Scheidemann, addressing soldiers and civilians
outside the Reichstag, in 1919. Despite the fiery oratorical
posture, there is no doubt that the fatal weakness of democracy under
the Weimar Republic can largely be attributed to the timidity and
conservatism of such leaders in 1918–19.

Soviet government actually organised the revolutionary wave. The
French and Italian Communist Parties were not founded until
December 1920 and January 1921 respectively, by which time the
wave was subsiding (although the Italians definitely derived inspiration from the Bolshevik example). In Germany, Rosa Luxemburg,
the leader of the Communist Party founded on the last day of 1918,
believed that Moscow's call for a new International was premature
and should await a spontaneous rising throughout Europe.

Rosa Luxemburg ardently praised the Bolshevik initiative and
advised the German workers to study Lenin's actions (of which she
was, however, not uncritical) in order to regain their own lost
capacity for historical action. Critical of the Mensheviks for having
clung to a coalition with the liberals (Cadets) in the summer of
1917, she insisted that every revolution must either advance at a
rapid tempo or fall back and disintegrate. She agreed with Trotsky
that the revolution must quickly assume international proportions
or perish, but the concept of a minority seizure of power violated
her deepest instincts. In the first days of 1919 a German revolution
could only be a minority revolution; Rosa Luxemburg was the
first to appreciate that the formation of the *Kommunistische Partei
Deutschlands* (KPD) did not automatically secure for it the support
of a majority of workers. The National Congress of Workers' and
Soldiers' Delegates, meeting in December, had overwhelmingly
preferred to Bolshevik extremism the policy canvassed by the
Sozialdemokratische Partei Deutschlands (SPD) and the left-wing
Independent Socialists (USPD) alike, of calling a democratically-
elected Constituent Assembly. It was against the advice of Rosa
Luxemburg and of Karl Liebknecht that the doctrinaire intellectuals of the KPD embarked in January upon the doomed revolutionary road which ended in the murder of them both.

Crushed in Berlin (and soon in Bavaria also) by the SPD government and by its chosen agents, the counter-revolutionary *Freikorps*,
the communists split following a vote on the question of partici-
pating in parliamentary elections – an activity which the Marxists
of the Second International had never challenged – and in the

reformist labour unions. In April 1920 a 'left' sectarian minority founded the German Workers' Communist Party which Lenin mocked as an 'infantile disorder,' as guilty of 'petty-bourgeois revolutionism' close to anarchism, as incapable of separating ends and means and of analysing each concrete situation. But the German Left was continuously recharging its revolutionary batteries. The Independents, disgusted by the barely reformist policy of the SPD and by its collusion with the old Imperial Army, broke up dramatically in October 1920, Ernst Thaelmann of Hamburg leading the left wing into the Communist Party. Two years later the right-wing rump jettisoned the last of its anti-reformist inhibitions and returned to the fold of the SPD.

Italy emerged from the war a defeated victor, disillusioned and exhausted, lynched by the contradictory forces of revolutionary socialism and nascent fascism, by the conflicting claims of a proletarian class and what the nationalists called a 'proletarian nation.' In October 1919 the PSI declared at Bologna that 'a revolutionary period has begun in which a profound transformation of society will lead from now on to the violent overthrow of bourgeois capitalist domination,' and urged that the workers' and peasants' councils – the Italian 'soviets' – be employed as the organs of socialist transformation. In 1920 the socialists gained a majority in twenty-four per cent of the communes and controlled thirty-six provincial councils. Expropriations of land began in July 1919 in the Romagna, then throughout northern Italy. Bombacci, the Vice-Secretary of the Socialist Party, published a draft soviet constitution. In 1920 the workers of Turin occupied the factories; the moment of truth had arrived; the revolutionary wave could either drive forward or disintegrate into sporadic violence. Both the PSI and the trade union confederation shrank from the final test and the workers foundered for lack of decisive leadership. In fact the Socialist Party was hesitant because divided. In March 1919 it had joined the Comintern *en bloc* in a fit of ill-considered enthusiasm and it was only later that it began to stumble over the most painful of the Comintern's twenty-one conditions for membership, the demand that the reformist wing be expelled. In January 1921, a left-wing faction led by Gramsci, Togliatti and Bordiga broke away impatiently and set up the Italian Communist Party. But the strike wave was already on the wane.

Social unrest in France at this period was somewhat less far-reaching than in either Germany or Italy. For one thing, it was confined to the workers alone; for another, it did not find expression in workers' councils or soviets and it faced a determined adversary in an overwhelmingly right-wing government and parliament. But it was by no means negligible; the workers responded to a fall in their standard of living by repeated strike actions. In the two years following the end of the war the SFIO membership grew fivefold, and by February 1920 the revolutionaries had gained the ascendency to the extent of withdrawing the Party from the Second International. A negotiating mission was sent to Moscow, a new strike wave gathered momentum, the government embarked upon arbitrary arrests, and in December a large majority of the SFIO adhered to the Comintern. But in France, as in Italy, the revolutionary momentum was played out.

In the years 1918–21 Communist Parties committed to an immediate revolution (which was not the same as attempting one) appeared throughout Europe, the most numerically powerful being those in Germany and Czechoslovakia.

The socialists

The issues which divided socialists from communists were basically three: reform or revolution; democracy or dictatorship; national independence or outside interference. Compelled to define its beliefs in relation to Bolshevism, the Second International explicitly equated democracy with parliamentary government, rejected revolutionary violence and committed itself to 'a reorganised society more and more permeated with socialism . . .' – the dream of Fabians everywhere. In adopting an unambiguously reformist programme at Heidelberg in 1925, German socialism embarked upon a course from which it was not to deviate in later years. In December 1963, the London *Times* paid this tribute to Erich Ollenhauer, the leader of the Party from 1952 until 1963. He helped, said *The Times*, to form 'a mildly progressive, highly respectable, and almost bourgeois party . . . if any reproach could be made to him, it was that, inevitably, by helping to transform German socialism and render it somewhat innocuous he made it almost indistinguishable from the more conservative political groups.'

In its devotion to parliamentary democracy and to constitutional processes, however, the British Labour Party was second to none. When the government failed to honour its pledge to break-off its military intervention against the Bolsheviks, rousing left-wing militants like Herbert Morrison to call for direct industrial action in the name of international working-class solidarity, Arthur Henderson spoke for the Labour leadership when he warned that unconstitutional minority action could prove to be an awkward precedent when the first Labour government was formed. Trotsky, casting his eagle eye on the British scene in 1925, mocked this view of politics as a game in which both sides abided by the rules, and

Erich Ollenhauer, Chairman of the German Social Democrats from 1952 until 1963. He represented a generation which had been forced into exile by Nazism and which found difficulty in making socialism attractive to the German electorate after the war. As a consequence, the doctrine of the Party came increasingly to resemble that of its conservative opponents.

likened the rejection of force to the rejection of gravitation. He had nothing but contempt for the religiosity of the pacifist Lansbury. J. H. Thomas' spirit of good fellowship with the employers, and Mrs Snowden's pious opinion that the Royal Family was overworked. The Labour Party remained unrepentant; it alone of the major European Socialist Parties rejected any pact with the extreme Left in the late 'thirties.

On the Continent practical reformism was constantly sustained by an articulate and rationalist theoretical revisionism. In Germany the ageing Kautsky and in Belgium Henri de Man elaborated and advanced in the light of the growth of totalitarian régimes and of recent psychological theories the work initiated thirty years earlier by Bernstein. In his *Au delà du Marxisme*, de Man looked forward in the best idealist tradition to a psychological metamor-

At the palace gates. Ramsay MacDonald, J. H. Thomas, Arthur Henderson
and J. R. Clynes, leading figures in the first Labour government, visit
Buckingham Palace in January 1924. Anxious to prove themselves respectable,
they tended to succumb to the ethos of the British 'establishment'.
While it is true that he lacked a majority in the House of Commons, MacDonald's
premiership was marked by excessive hesitancy and compromise.

phosis of habits and attitudes within all social groups, and he
urged socialists to adopt the democratic and Christian ideals betrayed by the bourgeoisie. Socialism must be a moral force; it
needed time and liberty, not violence. In France these views found
an echo in the Neo-Socialist movement.

But European socialism was not yet universally committed to reformism. In 1922, after the formation of the Italian Communist
Party, the PSI finally expelled its reformist wing and came peril-
ously close to joining the Comintern. Ten years later, the French
Socialist Party, faced with the development of neo-socialism within
its ranks, bravely declared its aim to be social revolution on the
basis of class struggle. In April 1933, Léon Blum denied that the
SFIO was in any sense reformist or participationist, a claim which
he reinforced by drawing a distinction between participation in

power (which he consistently rejected), the occupation of power on a defensive basis, and the conquest of power. The leader of a democratically-elected Popular Front government, Blum embarked in 1936 on the occupation of power. But when, in June 1937, his policy was thwarted by the Senate, it was only Zyromski and the left wing which favoured rallying popular support against the constitutional machinery, an action which must surely have entailed the conquest of power, whereas Blum, evidently afraid of civil war, not only resigned but decided to join the non-socialist Chautemps government – the participationist course he had hitherto rejected. The SFIO could not thereafter believe in its own revolutionary pretensions, and in 1939 an element of the left wing led by the quasi Trotskyist Marceau Pivert broke away to form the *Parti ouvrier et paysan*.

Of all the European Socialist Parties, the Spanish pursued perhaps the most curious course in the inter-war period. Its reformist tendency in the 'twenties can be attributed to a dual reaction: against the dictatorship of Primo de Rivera, and against the revolutionary extremism of the anarchists. At the moment of the

Left: Léon Blum, leader of the French Socialist Party between the wars. A strong opponent of the communists, he continued to affirm his devotion to the revolutionary ideal. *Opposite*: a huge demonstration protesting against an attack by rightist thugs on Blum. When he allowed the Senate to force the downfall of his Popular Front government in 1937, it became clear that he was not in fact a revolutionary.

establishment of the democratic Republic in 1931, the socialists aligned themselves with the left republicans (Azaña, Quiroga) on the moderate Left, as the defenders of a restrictedly political popular sovereignty against both the Right (which soon came to include Lerroux's right republicans) and the anarchists.

Spanish bourgeois democracy was doomed by the hostility of two powerful but opposing forces; the wealthy Right, upheld by the Church, and the anti-capitalist working class, supported by the rural poor. By 1934 the class war forced the socialists to collaborate with the anarchists in upholding the 40,000 Asturian miners who launched a revolutionary war, forming their own 'Red Army,' seizing the arms factories at Trubia and La Vega and resisting General Franco's Moors until they had nothing more with which to resist. Soon after the electoral victory of the Popular Front in 1936, the Left began to revert to its moderate and extremist wings, the republicans, right-wing socialists and, paradoxically, communists on one side, the left-wing socialists, the Trotskyist *Partido Obrero de Unificación* (POUM) and the anarcho-syndicalists on the other. On 24 May, Largo Caballero, the symbol of the new revolu-

The Spanish Civil War, 1936. The socialist Premier Largo Caballero (third from right) visits a Republican unit. The Popular Front had to cope with the immediate defection of most of the regular army to the rebel generals. At first each left-wing group formed its own militia units, but later, under communist influence, they were unified into a single Republican army. The communists and right-wing socialists combined to force out Largo Caballero in May 1937.

tionary spirit within the Socialist Party, inflamed the resentments of the anti-democratic Right by forecasting the imminent dictatorship of the proletariat. In May 1937, when he was finally ousted from the Premiership by the reformist forces within the republican camp, Largo Caballero was described by the anarchists, whom a few years earlier he had happily persecuted, as 'the most capable and honourable person for presiding over the government that must carry us to victory.'

The communists

At the moment of its birth, the Communist International was a revolutionary force. But not for long. The failure of the revolution in Germany, the evaporation of the strike waves in Italy and France, the failure of the Red Army's campaign against Poland, the Soviet Union's need for diplomatic and trading relations with the capitalist states, and, finally, the inauguration in Russia of the New Economic Policy – a tactical retreat from socialist construction – all these factors resulted in a radical reversal of the Comintern's revolutionary strategy in 1921. 'Had the Red Army taken Warsaw,' explained Zinoviev in 1922, 'the tactics of the CI today would be other than they are . . .'

The new 'united front' policy was essentially a defensive one, a technique of collaboration, of electoral pacts with the socialists, even of bringing to power socialist governments, which imposed an intolerable psychological strain on the European communists who had only one year earlier been encouraged to break utterly with the 'social chauvinists' and 'social traitors.' In the course of a single year (1921–2), the Italian and Czech Parties lost more than half their members, the French almost a half, and the German a third.

When in 1928 the Comintern arbitrarily reverted to a 'revolutionary' line, the Communist Parties were compelled to embark upon a sectarian policy which was as irrelevant to local conditions as it was dangerous. Stalin insisted that the whole movement should march in step with the swing to the left represented by the Five Year Plans, but such a correlation had no basis in necessity, only in dogmatism. The German Party headed for disaster; the exiled Italian communists played out the tragi-comedy of expelling from their skeleton ranks those 'opportunists' who wanted to perpetuate a broad, anti-fascist alliance. Certainly the period of capitalist stabilisation ended in 1929, but the Comintern made a fatal error in diagnosing the economic crisis which followed as revolutionary in its implications, rather than counter-revolutionary.

By 1935, communists were everywhere the most ardent apostles of a non-revolutionary popular front of all Left groups. In France, the communists had taken the initiative in exploring a basis for co-operation with the socialists and then, to the horror of the Marxists within the SFIO, of incorporating the bourgeois radicals into the fold. The motives were not exclusively domestic; the Soviet Union, threatened by Germany and Japan, and in search of collective security, was working now for an *entente* with the democracies.

The Left defeated. Republican militiamen laying down their arms
in a Madrid Square, watched by Nationalist soldiers,
in 1939. The Republicans held Madrid throughout the war,
but in the end German and Italian intervention on Franco's behalf,
combined with Anglo-French non-intervention on the Republic's behalf,
made defeat inevitable.

In complying more or less happily with these yogi-like contor-
tions, the communist does not cease subjectively to be a revolutionary. He is a Machiavellian; in every situation and every tactic,
defensive or aggressive, reformist or revolutionary, he sees himself
as an actor in a grand drama whose revolutionary outlines are
perfectly clear and indeed perfectly controlled by the master
dramatists in Moscow. Above all, he is convinced that the Soviet
Union must be defended at all costs and that the world revolution
depends on its survival.

History affords no more vivid example of communist adaptability to the exigencies of strategy than the Spanish Civil War. The
objective was clear: to encourage France and Britain to collaborate
with the Soviet Union in assisting the Republic militarily, and to
overcome bourgeois scruples about the Red Peril by pursuing as
conservative a domestic policy as possible, by insisting, as André
Marty put it in August 1936, that 'the present struggle in Spain is
not between capitalism and socialism but between fascism and
democracy.' Within a few months after the outbreak of the Civil
War, the CP, by making its position plain, had become the refuge
of 76,700 peasant proprietors and tenant farmers in search of
protection against collectivisation by anarchists and left socialists.
On 8 August, *Treball*, the communist organ in Catalonia, lamented
that small businessmen had 'hardly enough to eat ... because the
wages that they have to pay to the few workers they employ prevent
them from attending to their own daily needs ...'. The Party opposed any tendency towards agrarian collectivisation, wage
equality, the expropriation of factories by the workers themselves,
the granting of independence to Spanish Morocco – in short the
revolutionary policy which many, including George Orwell and
Trotsky, regarded as the indispensable dynamic for ultimate
victory. The exiled Trotsky, who had become the symbol of revolutionary Marxism, of 'permanent revolution,' and who had founded
a Fourth International to challenge the bureaucratic reformism of
the Third, described the right socialists and the communists in
Spain as 'Mensheviks of the first and second mobilisation.'

If the judgment was sound in 1937, it would have been equally sound in 1944–5, four years after Trotsky himself had been felled with an ice-axe in Mexico. Devotedly obedient to Moscow, all but the Yugoslav communists abandoned their hopes of an independent national revolution. In reality, the chances of an Italian revolution had been slender, but the French communists emerged from the Resistance struggle in an unprecedently favourable position and enjoying an unparalleled popularity. Their militia units, the *Francs-Tireurs*, took control of sizeable areas as the Germans withdrew. At Toulouse, Limoges, Montpellier and elsewhere local Party leaders exercised virtual dictatorships. But Stalin had decided upon a 'spheres-of-influence' policy of accommodation with the Western Powers; the possibility of a western revolution-from-below was sacrificed to the certainty of an eastern revolution-from-above. The French communist leader Maurice Thorez returned from Russia and ordered the Resistance units to disarm. The Liberation Committees, ideal instruments for a revolution, gave way to regular municipal administrations. If they still hoped

to gain power, the communists had to depend on the ballot box and on peaceful penetration. But three-quarters of the voters remained hostile.

Events in Italy followed a parallel course. Although Togliatti, who returned from Russia in April 1944, committed the Party to full co-operation with the war effort, the communist partisan units, the Garibaldi Brigades, were disarmed and the Allied Control Commission insisted that communists be kept out of the key ministries. Although its membership had risen to 2,250,000 by 1949, the only occasion on which the Party felt inclined to indulge in a display of strength was after the attempt on Togliatti's life in July 1948.

The Cold War inflicted on the communists a renewed and unrewarding isolation. But devotion to the Soviet Union and adamant opposition to the Atlantic Alliance by no means entailed a reversion to revolutionary tactics. In 1951 the British CP came out in

The face of Italian communism. In no West European country   103
does the Communist Party enjoy wider support than in Italy.
The picture shows Luigi Longo (now leader of the Party),
speaking in Rome in 1948 following an attempt on the life
of Palmiro Togliatti. On that occasion the working class
demonstrated a deep collective anger.

favour of the parliamentary road to socialism, and a year later the
review *Sondages* revealed that less than fifty per cent of communist
voters in France expected or desired a violent revolution, an attitude which the Party did nothing to combat. If the communists
remained the most violent of the left-wing parties, theirs had become a tactical violence, sporadic and limited in scope to sabotaging
the passage of war materials to Indo-China, demonstrating against
the arrival of a new NATO commander in Paris, or resisting a
threatened reduction in wages.

The anarchists

No discussion of the revolution-reform dichotomy within the Left
would be complete without reference to the movement which, in
the popular imagination if not in its own, became the very symbol
of lawless violence – anarchism. The anarchist, like the Marxist
but unlike the fascist, regards revolutionary force as the necessary
prelude to the elimination of every form of coercion. He looks
forward to a society in which no man shall raise his hand against
another and points to the state, the bastion of 'law and order,' as
the real source of violence. P.-J. Proudhon, the first of the really
influential anarchist writers, who was of this opinion, uttered contradictory statements on the desirability of violent struggle; on
occasion he condoned it but he did not systematically preach it.

It was with his Russian disciple Michael Bakunin that the
anarchist movement, whose basic concepts will be outlined in later
chapters, took an irrevocable turn towards revolutionary violence.
A romantic hero who took part in six insurrections, all of them
failures, a man of whom Herzen said that he had within him 'the
latent power of a colossal activity for which there was no demand,'
a martyr who for years was 'buried alive' in the Peter-Paul Fortress,
Bakunin, in his *Catechism of a Revolutionary*, depicted the true
revolutionist as cold, ruthless, single-minded, destructive and prepared to further the evils which would exhaust the people's
patience. In fact, Bakunin himself was neither cold nor destructive

by temperament, and the character of this curious document can undoubtedly be attributed to his notorious young disciple and collaborator, Nechaev.

Bakuninism first took root in Italy where ten anarchist federations, claiming over 26,000 members, existed by 1874. The Italian leaders Cafiero and Malatesta adopted Bakunin's revolutionary technique of propaganda by deed, the concept of drawing popular attention to the iniquitous nature of the system by direct action on the public stage. But the insurrectionary risings attempted in Italy in the 1870's were all dismal failures, some of them in the best traditions of musical comedy.

Disillusioned with the masses, the Black International Congress of 1881 inaugurated a phase of violent acts, as exotic as they were ineffective, by small groups of militants bearing names like *La Haine* (at Bordeaux) and *La Guerre Sociale* (at Toulon). The trial of the 'sixty-six' at Lyons in 1882 quickly castrated the anarchist organisation in France, although a lunatic fringe continued to challenge the social conventions and, on occasion, the borders of sanity. For some, like Sebastien Faure and the famous geographer Elisée Reclus, stealing was a revolutionary act, provided that the victim be properly selected. Servants were invited to poison their employers. In October 1881, one Emile Florian, intending to kill Gambetta but having failed to locate him, simply shot the first 'bourgeois' he encountered in the street.

Revolutionary terrorism was carried on in Russia by relatively large and organised groups; in France it was the work of individuals or tiny circles. Between March 1892 and June 1894 they were responsible for eleven dynamite explosions in Paris. The dynamiter Ravachol, who selected the house of a judge for his target, had several politically motiveless murders attributed to him, at least one of which could be confirmed. Yet the writer Paul Adam – certain French writers and post-Impressionist painters were strongly committed to anarchism in the 1890's – described him as '*le Renovateur du Sacrifice Essentiel.*' Vaillant, who threw a bomb into the Chamber of Deputies, was undoubtedly an idealist who had suffered an appalling life of misery and exploitation. To avenge his execution, Emile Henry committed the least lovely of the propagandist deeds when he hurled another bomb into the Café Terminus at the Gare Saint-Lazare, wounding twenty people and killing one. The anarchists were growing impatient with the masses whose apathy and servility rendered them accomplices of the tyrannical social system. But in general violence was directed against the symbols of state power. The record was statistically impressive: the Tsar assassinated in 1881, the French President in 1894, the Empress of Austria in 1898, the King of Italy in 1900, the President of the USA in 1901. The moral issue is difficult to evaluate. As Bernard Shaw pointed out, political violence is liable to have two faces; the upper classes cared less for a 'whiff of dynamite' than for the celebrated 'whiff of grapeshot.' When governments shed blood, as in 1848 or at the climax of the Paris Commune in 1871 when thousands were executed in cold blood, the action was either applauded or forgotten. Perhaps the main charge against the anarchist outrages is their total ineffectiveness.

In 1868 Bakunin despatched several of his disciples to Spain, one of whom, the Italian Fanelli, succeeded on his own initiative in inspiring an anarchist movement which by 1873 had about 50,000 supporters, mainly concentrated in the rural South. Among the peasants it took the form of a millenarian faith, moral, ascetic, redeeming, with every new strike, every church-burning, seen as heralding an imminent revolution, a single day of change which would usher in the good world. By the 1890's, the doctrine had taken root in the urban areas of Catalonia, and later, in a slightly more reformist form, within the trade unions grouped after 1910 in the *Confederación Nacional de Trabajo* (CNT). Barcelona was before and after the war the centre of anarchist violence and bourgeois counter-violence, a notable but not untypical incident being the shooting of the Archbishop of Saragossa by the anarchist leader Durutti in revenge for the murder of a CNT leader by police gunmen.

The mission of the FAI – the *Federación Anarquista Ibérica* –

founded in 1927, was to maintain the pure doctrine and to combat reformist tendencies within the mass organisation, the CNT. Inspired rather than assuaged by the establishment of the democratic Republic in 1931, the FAI, élitist militants in the Bakuninist tradition, embarked upon a new wave of violence, attempting a *putsch* in the Llobregat Valley near Barcelona in 1932, supporting and encouraging the Asturian miners in 1934, and joyously calling the revolutionary tune in Catalonia in the months following the outbreak of the Civil War.

There is no doubt that in Spain the anarchist revolutionary spirit and doctrine found mass support among the proletariat and were deliberately grafted on to the syndicalist labour unions. Revolutionary syndicalism often goes by the name of anarcho-syndicalism. But to what extent did this organic connection hold true in France in the decade preceding the First World War, the heroic period of the CGT? At first sight, a number of obvious connections suggest themselves. Syndicalism, like anarchism, was hostile to all political parties, abhorred the state, was economically collectivist or communist. Also, the political general strike may appear analagous to the individual act of terror, although its relative efficacy is bound to make it more functional and less exemplary. A number of leading French anarchists like Emile Pouget became ardent syndicalists, believing themselves to have developed rather than discarded their anarchist convictions. On the other hand, French syndicalism absorbed and redirected a wide variety of ideological currents, including Blanquism, and its *praxis* was evolved largely on the basis of a pragmatic response to daily experience. Papers like *Le Libertaire* and *L'Anarchie* remained hostile to syndicalism, and one of the leading historians of the French labour movement, Edouard Dolléans, has written that 'revolutionary syndicalism is as much a rupture with anarchism as with socialism.' This is doubtless an exaggeration, and the judgment certainly does not apply to Spain, but it serves as a reminder that syndicalism stood much closer to the mainstream of the French revolutionary tradition than did anarchism.

7 Democracy or dictatorship – or neither ?

The State: democrats and 'dictators'

Dictatorship, whatever its form or social content, is the negation of popular sovereignty. The Left, even when convinced of the necessity of a transitional dictatorship, invariably focuses its vision on some ideal of governmental democracy or of a society without government. Beyond the stormy mountains lie the sunlit plains. What emerges is a triple division: those for whom the Left must at all times be democratic; those absolute libertarians who regard democracy and dictatorship as equally damned in so far as they are manifestations of a single evil – state power; and those who see in a temporary dictatorship the unavoidable prelude to an ultimate condition which may be either democratic or libertarian. In general, the libertarians have complete faith in human nature and attribute strife and oppression to the existence of social *power*, whether political or economic. The democrats are more cautious about human nature but feel confident that men, given control of their own destinies, can improve institutions and laws in the interests of social justice. The 'dictators' are inclined to stress the practical obstacles to the immediate realisation of either ideal, obstacles such as a strong enemy, a backward economy, accumulated prejudice and ignorance, and so forth.

The Babouvists, who inherited the notion of the 'despotism of liberty' from the Jacobins, deduced the need for a dictatorship from two interdependent factors: the strength of the Right, and the people's inability to grasp at once 'the truth.' Before a people oppressed in mind and body could be capable of selecting the 'best' leaders, it must first be regenerated. Buonarroti reflected that if only Robespierre had been allowed a personal dictatorship, 'the Revolution would have attained its veritable end.' The conspirators, who planned to make of themselves an executive with the exclusive power to initiate legislation, were convinced that, 'a regenerator must take broad views. He must mow down all that impedes him, all that encumbers his path . . .'. Those found guilty of '*incivisme*' and of indolence would be consigned to forced labour. Ultimately, however, direct democracy, absolute popular control over the administration, would emerge as conflicting interests disappeared and social harmony based on communism was achieved. This central idea of a provisional élitist dictatorship was transmitted by Buonarroti to the revolutionaries of the 1830's, and particularly to Blanqui.

Blanqui, who was against too much idle speculation about the future society, but who inherited the Babouvist belief that 'the inevitable crown of civilisation' was communism, became the master apostle of the élitist dictatorship (to say 'practitioner' would be to ignore the fact that his political life was throughout clouded by failure). Impetuous by nature and impatient by conviction, he did not lack his moments of sober evaluation. Addressing the Central Republican Society on 26 February 1848, he anticipated Rosa Luxemburg's warning to the German communists in December 1918 when he asked: 'suppose we seized power by an audacious stroke ... who would answer for the duration of our power? ... What we need ... is the mass of the people, the faubourgs in insurrection, a new August 10th' (a reference to 1792). But such moods did not last long. In 1839, in 1848 and again in October 1870 he seriously exaggerated the degree of popular support that an 'audacious stroke' would arouse.

He had no time for parliamentary democracy. Revolutionary Paris must take the law into its own hands. In March 1848 he urged the adjournment of the national elections which he knew would prove fatal to the cause of socialism, if not to the Republic itself. He pointed out that the country people, whose meagre primary education had long been guided by the enemies of the Republic, would prefer their local squires to the republican leaders of whom they as yet knew little or nothing. Among his contemporaries, Blanqui's faith in dictatorship was by no means unique. Barbès and Weitling shared it, as did the French communist exiles in London. For these men, still living in the shadow of the Jacobin experience, reason shone bright and hard as steel.

Less doctrinaire and more empirical, but equally disenchanted with the vision of the people as the agents of their own liberation,

Garibaldi discovered the full extent of peasant inertia, cowardice and egoism during his unorthodox military exploits in the 1860's in the cause of a united Italy. Landing at the head of his famous Thousand in Sicily in May 1860, he at once proclaimed himself dictator and personally appointed governors for all twenty-four districts of the island. Trusted, and even worshipped, by the people to an amazing degree, his word was automatically law. Later he ruled Naples as dictator for two months and introduced a number of left-wing projects, such as land reform and free education, which were not destined to be implemented. A decade later Garibaldi remained committed to the idea of a dictator elected by the people with a mandate to exercise full power for a two year period – a project almost as naïve as it was sincere. 'I am still in favour of honest dictatorship,' he wrote in 1871, 'which I consider the only antidote for eradicating the cancers of this corrupt society . . .' In another backward, peasant-dominated society, Russia, certain Populists like Tchakev were coming afresh to the conclusion reached by the democrat Pavel Pestel, that a revolutionary élite must seize and provisionally exercise power on behalf of the masses.

Babeuf, Blanqui, Garibaldi, Pestel and Tchakev all differed from Marx in their advocacy of the élitist or one-man dictatorship and in the fact that their thought was conditioned by a pre-industrial or semi-industrial society in which a physically dispersed and politically immature peasantry had not yet given birth to a physically co-ordinated and politically advanced proletariat. Babeuf was aware of the exploitation of the '*petits*' (almost everyone) by the '*gros*' (about 1,000,000), but he had no clearly defined view of social stratification or of the complexity of class struggle. Blanqui thought in terms of Paris, of the metropolis, and not of the nascent provincial proletariat. For Garibaldi and Tchakev the people and the peasants were almost synonymous.

With the advent of Marxism the emphasis shifts to the dictatorship of a class, of the proletariat. Engels wrote to Bebel in 1875: 'so long as the proletariat still *uses* the state, it does not use it in the interests of freedom but in order to hold down its adversaries . . .'.

The young Marx addressing a meeting.

But the exact nature of the dictatorship as envisaged by Marx is far from clear. In the *Communist Manifesto* (1848) and the Erfurt Programme (1891) it appears in the guise of a Jacobin-democratic republic; in *The Class Struggles in France* (1848–50) and *The Eighteenth Brumaire* (1852), as a centralised dictatorship without formal representation; in *The Civil War in France* (1871), as a libertarian federation of communes. These literary mutations were largely the reflection of the shifting pattern of events; Marx obviously believed the problem would be solved by circumstances.

There can be no doubt that he envisaged the eventual disappearance of the proletarian state and, with it, of the state as such. 'There will,' he wrote, 'no longer be political power . . . since political power is precisely the official summary of the antagonism in civil society.' Engels insisted that their differences with the anarchists were purely technical, not a question of *whether* the classless, stateless society would emerge, but *how* and *when*:

> The proletariat seizes the state power and transforms the means of production in the first instance into state property. But in doing this, it puts an end to itself as the proletariat . . . it puts an end also to the state as the state . . . the interference of the state power in social relations becomes superfluous in one sphere after another . . . the state is not 'abolished', it *withers away*.

Whether Marx and Engels were convinced that a complex society, even a communist one, was compatible with the complete absence of authority, as the anarchists insisted that it was, is not quite clear. In 1875 Marx wrote of 'the future state organisation of the communist society,' without elaborating the point.

The anti-dictatorial currents flowed powerfully to challenge the dictatorial. With the partial exception of the later Jacobin purists, radicals and republicans everywhere called for a democracy based on parliamentary government. The economic Left was more attracted to dictatorship than the political Left; among the latter, the Jacobins were a solitary exception. Throughout Europe the non-socialist Left worked with a single mind for parliamentary democracy. In England, the Chartists and the Benthamite radicals favoured it; in France Lamartine and the moderate republicans along with Ledru-Rollin and the Montagnards; in Italy, Mazzini. But faith in democracy was to be found also in the socialist ranks; Louis Blanc and Lassalle shared with certain Chartist leaders confidence that the proletariat could harness democracy to its own advantage by sheer force of numbers, although in such cases a certain amount of class co-operation would be necessary. The Fabians feared the potential power of even a democratic, socialist state to such a degree that they canvassed the virtues of a parliament divided into political and social departments. Bernstein naturally denounced all dictatorships. Kaustky subscribed to the orthodox Marxist historical progression, but he was deeply anti-pathetic to anything that savoured of a Blanquist or élitist tyranny, and it was on precisely this issue that he fell out with Lenin and Trotsky after the Bolshevik revolution. He, like Bernstein, could see in Bolshevism only a new militarism, anti-democratic and thereby implicitly counter-revolutionary.

The dilemma of democracy or dictatorship, like that of revolution or reform, was not solved by circumstantial factors alone; doctrine and temperament were equally important in both cases. In any single society, contradictory voices could be heard; Marx and Lassalle in Germany, Guesde and Jaurès (who would not countenance a single-party state) in France, Lazzari and Turati in Italy. Nevertheless, within the 'dictatorial' school there was evidence of a correlation between the economic and social structure on the one hand and the type of dictatorship envisaged on the other. The correlation was never an absolute one because doctrinal and temperamental factors also intervened.

The divergence is well illustrated by a controversy conducted between Lenin and Rosa Luxemburg, the one working in an as yet predominantly peasant economy, the other in a fully industrialised Germany. Lenin agreed that the state would wither away, and that there 'will vanish all need for force, for the subjection of one man by another . . .'. But the Russian Marxists had to face the fact that their own proletariat would not for many years constitute the vast majority of the population; consequently proletarian coercion would have to be different from what Marx had predicted not only in degree but also in kind. The Bolshevik Nikolai Bukharin departed radically from the spirit of Marx when he wrote that, 'proletarian coercion, in all its forms, from executions to forced labour, is, paradoxical as it may sound, the method of moulding communist humanity out of the human material of the capitalist period.'

For Rosa Luxemburg such a conception of the proletarian dictatorship was not merely 'paradoxical,' as Bukharin put it, but a denial of Marxism itself. Despite the *putschist* temptations afforded

Below left: Trostky, seen at a Red Army parade.
As People's Commissar for War, Trotsky
played a leading role in organising the victory
of the Reds over the Whites in the civil war of 1918–20.
Below right: Lenin at home, 1922. Already a sick man,
he had less than two years to live.

in Germany by the political chaos following the armistice and by the temporary paralysis of the bourgeoisie, she wrote in *Rote Fahne* on 18 November 1918: 'the Spartacus League (the nucleus of the future Communist Party) will never take power in any other way than through the clear, unambiguous will of the great majority of the proletarian masses in all Germany . . .' She criticised sharply the Bolsheviks' action in dissolving the Constituent Assembly (in which they were a minority) in January 1918, in destroying the freedom of the press and in putting restrictions on free association. 'Freedom only for the supporters of the government, only for

The lighter side of anarchism. Sunday evening at the Anarchists' Club in Berners Street, London. Cries of 'Awake, ye men who toil', and 'Up, proletarians!', were followed by groans for the capitalists and cheers for Karl Marx (indicating some confusion). In the 1890's anarchists in the Latin countries caused some bloodshed. Bernard Shaw contrasted their 'whiff of dynamite' with Napoleon's 'whiff of grapeshot'. Not everyone saw the joke.

members of one party – however numerous they may be – is no freedom at all.' She preferred class dictatorship, the constant activity of the masses, what she called 'unlimited democracy,' to 'the dictatorship of a handful of politicians . . . in the sense of the rule of the Jacobins.'

It was, perhaps, easy to criticise. Nevertheless hers was the only conception of a socialist dictatorship which could have any relevance to West European conditions, and it has been one of the fundamental weaknesses of the Communist Parties that, in oscillating between the call for a Leninist dictatorship and no dictatorship at all, they have consistently relegated Rosa Luxemburg, who had the temerity to challenge the Bolsheviks, to oblivion. In recent years it has become increasingly difficult to discern what kind of dictatorship, if any, these parties do in fact envisage. During the Spanish Civil War, the CP successfully poured cold water on Largo Caballero's talk of proletarian dictatorship; in 1946 Thorez remarked that if he became Premier, there would be no dictatorship in France; in 1951 the British Party officially abandoned this aspect of Marxism and virtually gave up the ghost.

Anarchists and the state

For anarchists, the answer has always been quite simply – neither. The state in any form is inherently tyrannical and must be replaced by some form of non-governmental co-operation between free individuals and groups. For Proudhon, the Jacobins, Bonapartists. democratic republicans and state socialists were all equally damned as worshippers of the state. As for universal suffrage, it was '*une vraie lotterie*.' The future of humanity lay in a private mental construction of his own, in the substitution of what he called 'commutative justice' and 'the reign of contracts' for 'distributive justice' and 'the reign of laws.' Contract would replace authority; each group, commune or economic corporation should be formed by contract among its members and considered as an independent moral entity, dealing with all other groups on equal

terms. 'This,' he wrote, 'would be exactly as if my will repeated itself *ad infinitum*.'

Bakunin accepted Proudhon's hostility to the state. The International Brotherhood which he organised in Italy subscribed to his opinion that, 'the state is authority; it is force . . . Even when it commands what is good, it hinders and spoils it, just because it commands it, and . . . excites the legitimate revolts of liberty . . .' In 1872 he, Malatesta, Cafiero, Costa and their brethren passed a resolution to the effect that the proletariat must destroy all forms of political power and not set up its own dictatorship. The most intellectually formidable exposition of the libertarian case, however, is to be found in the work of another exiled Russian, Peter Kropotkin.

Marx regarded political structures as evolving dialectically in reflection of economic forms and class interests. Kropotkin abstractly separated two historical tendencies, the Roman, imperialist and

authoritarian on the one hand, and the popular, federalist and libertarian on the other. Described in this way, divorced from context, each tendency must represent not an unconscious evolution but a state of mind, an attitude, the one oppressive, the other 'natural' and good. Good and Evil, the eternal actors in the ethical cycle, return to dominate the stage of recorded history, decked out in a number of 'period' costumes. For Marx, Babeuf's communism was immature; for Kropotkin, its author had to be morally condemned as 'the first theoretician of centralised socialism, of state socialism.'

In Spain, and particularly in Catalonia, the anarchist movement made periodic compromises without forfeiting its basic libertarian

'An anarchist meeting', *c.* 1897, by Picasso.
Between the political *avant-garde* in France
and the literary and artistic *avant-garde* there
existed close personal ties in the 1890's.

117

intransigence. In 1910, at a time of acute class war, anarchists stifled their prejudices to the extent of voting in support of a radical-socialist coalition. But it was the Civil War which provided the supreme test, an acute tension between doctrine and efficacy, between hostility to all political parties in search of state power and even greater hostility to the Nationalists, the military enemy. In September 1936, anarchists joined the local government at Barcelona while calling it a 'Regional Defence Council.' Soon after, in an attempt to protect their achievements against the hostility of the Madrid government, four anarchists decided, without consulting the rank and file, to join it, accepting the ministries of Health, Industry, Commerce and Justice. As a result they not only violated their most cherished principles but also became more than ever prisoners of a situation in which their own committees were being replaced by regular provincial and municipal councils and their own presses, papers and radio in Catalonia were being suppressed by the Soviet-controlled GPU. But the anarchists were not always on the receiving end of violence and coercion. In the early months of the war the anarchist militia units like the notorious Durutti column left in their crusading wake a trail of bloodshed and slaughter, many of their victims being humble peasants who were executed on the basis of suspicion or hearsay.

Party structure

The argument over 'democracy or dictatorship' ramifies in more than one direction. There is, for example, a close, if not an absolute correlation between a party's theoretical position on the future society and its own internal structure. Babeuf, whose faith in spontaneous popular risings had been destroyed by the defeat of the *sans-culottes* in Prairial 1795, was, like Blanqui after him, an integral élitist. The conspiracy of 1796 took the form of an organised, disciplined and clandestine plot supervised by an all-powerful Insurrectionary Committee. Bolsheviks and Mensheviks, not surprisingly, carried their dispute into the realm of party organisation;

for many, indeed, this was the main dispute. The Mensheviks, convinced that Russia must experience the full cycle of bourgeois democracy before the socialist revolution could be so much as countenanced, naturally favoured a mass organisation run on open, democratic lines. Lenin, on the other hand, always alert for the revolutionary situation which would bring to power a proletarian minority, judged the problem purely in terms of efficiency, insisting that the model revolutionary party must be led by a corps of trained, professional revolutionaries, blending within their ranks 'agitators,' like Bebel and Guesde, and 'propagandists,' like Kautsky and Lafargue. Certainly, agreed Lenin, organisation and secrecy ran counter to pure democracy; but what use was an open and fully publicised party against the Tsarist police?

In 1918 Rosa Luxemburg criticised the Leninist state; in 1904 she had criticised the Leninist party. In her *Leninism and Marxism*, she took issue with his *One Step Forward, Two Steps Backward*, in which he argued that the central committee, the élite, should nominate all local party committees; the reverse, in fact, of the elective process. 'Such centralism,' she wrote, 'is a mechanical transposition of the organisational principles of Blanquism into the mass movement of the socialist working class.'

'Leninist centralism,' the basic method of organisation adopted within the Communist International and its member parties, visualised a dual process; the base, the militants in their cells, elects the head indirectly through a series of hierarchical layers; the head then commands the base and the base obeys unquestioningly. Lenin himself was anxious to stress the democratic aspect of this procedure and to dispel the widespread impression that Moscow dictated to other parties. 'All this clamour about Moscow "dictatorship" etc., is simply a red herring. As a matter of fact, of the twenty members of the Communist International Executive Committee, only five belong to the Russian Communist Party.' But a statistical *riposte* such as this missed the point; the essence of the Moscow dictatorship was its quasi-voluntary acceptance by powerful factions of supporters and agents within the foreign CP's, militants who believed that there was no alternative but to follow the lead of the first socialist state.

'Discipline' became the watchword. An early incident, the first of many, illustrates its rapid ascendency over all other factors, doctrine included. In March 1921 a communist rising was attempted in Germany on the initiative of the Comintern and its agent Bela Kun. The Secretary of the KPD, Paul Levi, condemned the manoeuvre as a meaningless and dangerous anarchistic *putsch*. For this he was expelled. Lenin made it known privately that Levi's analysis had in fact been correct, but that insubordination had to be penalised. The subsequent history of the German Party, the most important outside Russia until 1933, illustrates the progressive extinction of inner-party democracy which discredited the whole Comintern apparatus in its early years. When in 1924 the left wing gained control of the KPD on a more or less democratic basis, Stalin and his agent Manuilsky set to work to reverse the balance, carefully channelling funds through the Soviet embassy in Berlin to obedient functionaries like W. Pieck and H. Eberlein. By 1926–7 a state of siege prevailed; the opposition could no longer gain a hearing in the Party press, minority reports were suppressed, cell meetings cancelled. The left wing was expelled at the Essen Congress in 1927. Bukharin, temporarily and precariously at the head of the Comintern, commented on the developing situation: 'if you drive out all the intelligent people who are not very pliable, and keep only obedient idiots, you will certainly ruin the Party.' But things got worse. Discipline was the better enforced by introducing into the normal structure of workshop and district cells four or five additional '*Apparats*,' independent cadres run by Comintern or GPU agents. Two slogans reverberated everywhere: 'the front line is no place for discussions'; and 'wherever a communist happens to be, he is always in the front line.'

The malaise was not confined to Germany alone. Stalinism was dogmatically universalist, systematically militarist, or it was nothing. The statutes of the Comintern, which called for annual congresses, were observed until 1922 but thereafter the gaps grew

120

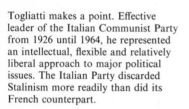

Togliatti makes a point. Effective leader of the Italian Communist Party from 1926 until 1964, he represented an intellectual, flexible and relatively liberal approach to major political issues. The Italian Party discarded Stalinism more readily than did its French counterpart.

longer, silencing the militants and devolving power increasingly on the oligarchy in Moscow. After 1924 there was a four year gap: after 1928 a seven year gap; after 1935 no congress was held before the formal dissolution of the Comintern in 1943. Analysis of the ultimate fate of the members and candidate members of the Executive Commission of the Comintern from 1919 until 1943 reveals that approximately half their number were either expelled from the movement or died as a result of the Stalinist purges.

In the French Party, elective processes were gradually reduced to a mere formality and the practice of co-option increasingly prevailed. Changes take place only when a fratricidal power-struggle develops among the leaders. Maurice Thorez, elected General Secretary in 1930, was at the helm until 1964. In Italy, Togliatti's reign was even longer. In a period of over forty years, less than thirty people sat on the Political Bureau of the British CP. All this could the more easily be attributed to the need for vigilance and discipline in an undoubtedly hostile society, were it not for its remarkable resemblance to the current practice in the Soviet Union.

Within the democratic Left, the inner-party structure tends to be correspondingly more democratic and the freedom of discussion more marked. Here, as in the democratic state itself, the general will or the majority principle are most likely to be deformed by the growth of bureaucratic oligarchies with a vested interest in self-perpetuation. The French Socialist Party has always found it difficult to control its own parliamentary deputies, who are liable to seduction by '*la République des camarades*' and whose contribution from their salaries to the Party exchequer at one time gave them an undemocratic influence and freedom of action.

In Germany, obedience was a habit. Lassalle, although a democrat, argued that a workers' organisation must follow its chief blindly and serve as a hammer in his hands. The pre-1914 SPD, whether committed to parliamentary democracy or to the dictatorship of the proletariat, could hardly invoke either ideal as justification for its unique susceptibility to what Robert Michels called 'the law of the accumulation of functions.' A single socialist might serve in a triple capacity, as a town-councillor, a member of the provincial Diet, and as a Reichstag deputy. Or he might combine his functions as a labour union secretary with those of a newspaper editor. Marked fluctuations in the membership of socialist sections contributed to the growth of oligarchy. In 1906, forty-seven per cent of the Munich section had been members for less than two years, and seventy-two per cent for less than four years. Apathy or lack of stamina among the many have always been the main allies of the ambitious few. Also, the Party bureaucrat of working class origin who had risen in affluence and status through the Party's administrative and clerical apparatus possessed no skill which would provide a comparable standard of living in the event of his deposition. The bureaucracy naturally nursed and defended its interests with devotion.

Half a century later, bureaucracy had become no less prominent a feature of the German socialist scene. Delegates to Party conferences were chosen by district committees closely controlled by paid functionaries. After 1948, Party conferences became biennial instead of annual. Ollenhauer's position in the machine made him the almost inevitable successor to Schumacher in 1952; a jealous oligarchy of veteran officials of Weimar vintage was not calculated to offer the most dynamic of appeals to the young. The British

Labour Party is certainly democratic, but even here the leader, the potential Prime Minister, is elected by the 'Parliamentary Party' alone, and not by the annual Conference. Aneurin Bevan, a hero to Party militants, narrowly escaped expulsion from the Parliamentary Party, and in 1960 Hugh Gaitskell, as leader, made it clear that he considered it to be his privilege not only to fight but also to defy Conference's decisions if he thought fit.

Libertarian in their aspirations, the anarchists have generally remained staunchly libertarian in their daily practice. But not invariably; the consciousness of the need to fight a hostile system with its own weapons which dominated Babeuf, Blanqui and Lenin has, on occasion, also percolated into the anarchist mind. Bakunin's International Brotherhood was notably hierarchical and élitist in structure, designed to meet organised force with organised force. His Russian disciple Nechaev founded his terrorist group on the strictest disciplinary basis and went to the length of having a student follower murdered for a suspected act of indiscipline.

In France there existed no organised anarchist movement, only small and intensely voluntarist groups. In rural Spain, and particularly in Andalusia, hedge-preachers and village prophets carried the libertarian ideal to all who cared to listen in an atmosphere of open debate and discussion. The Spanish anarchists remained as good as their word; an English communist who fought in the Civil War complained that 'previous experience had shown that any argument with anarchists would pass through all the debating levels to a national conference, and then no results would be achieved.' Lack of discipline was most marked in those anarchist columns where the leadership was on an elective and temporary basis. Military disasters ensued, and on 7 August 1936 *Solidaridad Obrera*, the leading organ of the CNT, was compelled to denounce 'a liberty which in many cases degenerates into wantonness'. Perhaps the last word rests with the anarchist writer Gaston Leval who remarked that it was impossible for a true libertarian to fight a war because 'war and anarchism are two conditions of humanity that are mutually repugnant.'

8 Beyond capitalism

The pre-socialist Left

It was the logic of events rather than any preconceived theory which led the Jacobins to join combat not only with the royalist aristocracy but also with the conservative and pro-Girondin bourgeoisie. Neither Robespierre nor Saint-Just regarded Jacobinism as a hammer wielded by the wage-earners to smash private property. The Montagnard Convention made no attempt to repeal the *loi Le Chapelier* of 1791 which prohibited all associations of workers and employers, all collective bargaining, strikes and workers' meetings. The Jacobins developed their economic policy pragmatically, dealing with the poorer classes in the capacity of champion, relieving officer or policeman as the situation seemed to dictate.

In Britain, where industrial capitalism was already more advanced and where a clear-cut conflict between employers and workers could no longer be concealed, the democratic radicals adopted an even more detached view of the proletarian condition in the light of the current economic orthodoxy of Malthusian *laissez-faire*. Francis Place, who described all legislative interference with the workings of the economy as 'pernicious,' declared coldly: 'the law must compel the observance of compacts. There it should end. So long as the supply of labour exceeds the demand, the labourer will undersell his fellows.' Thus for the early political Left, capitalism, private enterprise, was the single rational form of economic activity. It was as absurd to contend that the people had the right to extend their sovereignty to the economic sphere by expropriation or control as it was to claim that they had the right to regulate the orbits of the moon. It was not a question of rights but of natural, mechanical and self-adjusting laws with which it was perilous to interfere.

Yet Jacobin economic policy began to assume a frightening logic. In April 1793, Robespierre observed that 'the right of private property, like all other rights, is limited by the obligation to respect the rights of others,' a formula no less significant for its ambiguity, and he went on to support a tax graduated according to wealth.

Gracchus Babeuf,
the first revolutionary
communist activist of
the modern period.

The Montagnards had few qualms about controlling prices and wâges and imposing additional taxes and forced loans on the rich for the duration of the war. If the principle is admitted as relevant to an emergency, it is nevertheless admitted and in the course of time it will be extended. Tom Paine, who distinguished between legitimate and illegitimate forms of wealth, attacked the monopolistic wealth of the great landed proprietors which he saw as an affront to justice and a threat to democracy. The extreme wing of the political Left halted only at the doorstep of socialism. Hébert remarked that 'everywhere and in all times men of commerce have had neither heart nor soul; their cash-box is their god; they only know how to thieve and deceive . . . (but) nothing is more respectable than a patriotic merchant . . . I have known many businessmen who were the fathers of their workers . . . Unfortunately such characters are rare, but the Republic will produce more, I hope.'

In so far as the Jacobins harboured a coherent social ideal, it was one of a community of small but independent farmers and artisans, frugal, virtuous – the best guarantors of democracy. This model was later adopted by the Chartist leader Feargus O'Connor and, on an anarchist basis, by Proudhon. An enemy of communism, O'Connor believed in 'mine and thine,' in giving each man as much land as he could profitably cultivate. Lammenais was opposed to economic collectivism; Mazzini wanted society to transcend the class war, to harmonise property with the common interest; the Montagnard leader Ledru-Rollin looked forward to a time when private property would be made available to all. The political Left insisted that human virtue, if given free expression through democratic channels, would limit inequalities to the minimum required by individual initiative and self-fulfilment.

Anti-capitalism

The fifty-odd years which reached their climax and anti-climax in the revolutions of 1848 witnessed the growth of a more extreme attitude inclined to regard capitalism and popular sovereignty as

incompatible and, consequently, to advocate that the people, the producers, take control of the economy. Babeuf developed to a socialist conclusion the anti-capitalist bias expressed three years earlier by Hébert. 'Speculators and merchants league together to hold the real producer at their mercy, so as to be always in a position to tell him: work hard, eat little, or you will not eat at all. That is the barbarous law dictated by the capitalists.' In Britain, Charles Hall was the first to attempt a statistical demonstration of the injustices of capitalism. Reacting against the conclusions, yet at the same time accepting the premises of Ricardo and the classical economists who argued that the 'natural' price of labour was its maintenance at subsistence level, writers like Hall and Thomas Hodgskin concluded that under capitalism wages could never rise above subsistence level and that reform agitation within the system was futile. In his *Labour Defended Against the Claims of Capital* (1825), Hodgskin wrote: 'it is the overwhelming nature of the demands of capital, sanctioned by the laws of society, enforced by the legislature, and widely defended by political economists, which keep, which ever have kept, and which ever will keep, as long as they are allowed . . ., the labourer in poverty and misery.'

According to the employers and to their priests, the political economists, to raise wages was to lower profits and so reduce the capital available for investment. The demand for labour decreases and wage levels collapse disastrously. Poverty, then, is nature's medicine. It was not until later that a more mature theory recognised and acknowledged that higher wages would stimulate consumption, so increasing the demand for labour and raising wage levels. By its failure to perceive and to act on this principle, early capitalism became the godfather of socialism.

Anti-capitalism, like industrial capitalism itself, developed rather later in France than in Britain. Babeuf's had been a lone voice crying in the wilderness, an anachronism which historians have found easier to describe than to explain. But by 1845 the journal *l'Atelier* was complaining of 'the chain binding us to capital,' Louis Blanc had already formulated his own critique and Proudhon was beginning to describe the physical and mental degradation of the workers and the strangulation of peasants and artisans alike by high interest rates and high rents.

Karl Marx derived much of his initial information about the actual effects of capitalism on human beings from Engels, whose *Condition of the Working Class in England* (1844) constituted a devastating indictment of the pioneering capitalist mentality. While it is true that Engels was mistaken in assuming that the workers' standard of living was lower in the 1840's than in the previous two decades, and lower also than that of the pre-industrial craftsmen, and while he may have tended to minimise the importance of recent legislation limiting hours of work for women and children in textile factories and illegalising their employment underground in the mines – while this has to be admitted, Engels nevertheless revealed and depicted an appalling situation. Experience showed that each new technical invention resulted in unemployment, want and crime. Machines could be handled by women and children at lower wages; in 1844 Ashley revealed that adult males over eighteen comprised

Punch cartoon in anticipation of the Great Exhibition of 1851. Mr Punch suggests to Prince Albert another exhibition displaying some different products of the industrial revolution. Marx and Engels gathered their material on the inhuman aspects of early capitalism mainly from the English scene.

less than one-quarter of the total factory labour force. Family ties were broken, children whose mothers were working a twelve or thirteen hour day lacked proper care. Disease, deformity and squalor surrounded the booming factories. If industrial accidents were frequently caused by the carelessness of the victims, then who, asked Engels, was to blame if not the class which kept them mentally retarded? And even if there had not been an absolute decline in the proletarian standard of living in the period 1790–1840, the working class share of the national wealth had fallen sharply when compared to that of the bourgeosie, generating an acute psychological sense of grievance.

Marx and Engels regarded capitalism as a dynamic force bound by its own internal logic to concentrate exclusively on profits and

128

so, through increased automation, constantly to depress wages. Large monopolies would crush the smaller businesses: 'the lower strata of the middle class sink gradually into the proletariat . . .' for two basic reasons; lack of capital; and the obsolescence of specialised skills resulting from new techniques of mass production. Capitalism produces the large class that must inevitably destroy it, thus begetting, in the language of dialectics, 'its own negation.' Capitalism was doomed not because it was immoral but because it was irrational and prey to its own contradictions. 'The essence of bourgeois society consists precisely in this, that *a priori* there is no conscious social regulation of production. The rational and naturally necessary asserts itself only as a blindly working average.' The market being able to correlate production and consumption only in a haphazard manner, surplus capital is destroyed in periodic upheavals and crises. In 1877 Engels wrote; 'we have now experienced it five times since 1825, and at the moment we are experiencing it for a sixth time.'

Marx naturally tended to discount the possibilities of far-reaching reforms. It is undeniable that the antithesis between the profit motive and the worker's wage-hunger has never been resolved, but capitalism has on the whole learned that wages represent buying power, increased production and future profits. For Marx capitalism was a demoniac force and the capitalist himself not an independent, flexible fellow but the mesmerised embodiment of this force. In 1875 he wrote: 'a general prohibition of child labour is incompatible with the existence of large-scale industry and hence an empty, pious aspiration.' He meant, of course, capitalist industry. Such narrow dogmatism was partly the result of an intense moral indignation which he and Engels vainly tried to disguise under the formal trappings of 'science.' This underlying moralism is well illustrated by his central thesis on 'value' according to which commodities have objective values dependent on the amount of labour embodied in them. Yet market prices are invariably higher. The difference, 'surplus value,' is pocketed by the capitalist or middleman and in this way the worker is exploited. The notion that

Left: Proudhon, author of the much-misunderstood phrase 'property is theft'. The cartoon depicts him trying to destroy it. In reality, he firmly upheld the principle of limited private property against Marxian socialism.

Right: National Workshops (tailors) in the prison of Clichy, Paris, in 1848. The workshops were run in such a way by the Provisional Government as deliberately to excite bourgeois animosity. They did not last long.

labour regulates value is a healthy moral theory, but it is not susceptible to proof. On the contrary, it is a highly subjective moral viewpoint likely to appeal to large sections of the working class.

By Lenin's time it was beyond casuistry to substantiate Marx's prediction of the progressive pauperisation of the mass of the population. Lenin, in fact, complained about the appearance of a reformist 'proletarian aristocracy,' an indication of a contrary process. He did, however, develop one aspect of the Marxist critique by drawing attention to the growth of huge monopolies which not only exploited the colonial peoples directly, by expropriating surplus value, but also exploited the European masses indirectly by committing them to predatory wars in which they had nothing to gain and everything to lose. 'Germany,' he wrote in 1915, 'is *governed* by not more than 300 magnates of capital, and the number of these is constantly diminishing.' If this argument had some foundation, the reality was far more complex.

Socialist systems

Against this backcloth of a developing anti-capitalism, we may examine briefly the various alternative systems advocated by the economic Left. For the purposes of description, these systems can be classified into three broad categories: the mutualist, the socialist

and the communist. In practice various hybrids have resulted from cross-fertilisation and also from the adaptability of each category to either a state-orientated or a libertarian interpretation.

Mutualism is the form of socialism (and there are grounds for doubting whether it can be categorised as a socialism at all) having most in common with capitalism. Proudhon, the intellectual father of mutualism, was the man who wrote, 'property is theft.' But he referred only to capitalist property, the product of unjust accumulation and exploitation, and not to private property as such. Communism, for Proudhon, was slavery. Twenty-four million French peasants would never, he insisted, submit to socialism, to what he derided as the 'dogma of association'; indeed had they not applauded the repression of the Parisian workers in June 1848 as representing the repression of communism?

Proudhon, then, wanted neither capitalism nor socialism but the redistribution of the land to the agricultural producers and the creation of a land credit bank providing these producers with easy credit at reduced interest rates repayable by annuities. Here is to be found the socialistic element in mutualism – cheap social credit. Labour would be divided not by 'castes' but by industries; commerce would be based on mutual contracts; equilibrium would be established between values and properties. 'The contract resolves all problems. The producer deals with the consumer, the associated worker with his company, the peasant with his commune, the commune with the canton . . .' If thus condensed Proudhon's proposals appear nebulous, the fact is that in their totality they were not only nebulous but vulnerable to logical criticism. How the mutualist system was to resist a renewed degeneration into acquisitive capitalism he did not make clear, and most of his protective stipulations were designed to ward off socialism rather than capitalism. He favoured competition ('*concurrence*') and insisted, moreover, that '*la propriété, c'est la libre disposition.*' Yet a free market is the first condition of a capitalist economy.

Inconsistent a doctrine as mutualism may have been, it provided the inspiration for numerous co-operative production societies which were set up on private initiative in France in the 1860's, although the attempt to create a credit bank failed and was deferred until after the 'revolution.' Tolain and his colleagues in the trade associations carried the doctrine into the First International where it fought a losing battle with Marxism and collectivism.

The term 'socialist' is first found in the issue of the London *Co-operative Magazine* for November 1827, while its first recorded use in a French paper occurred in 1832 in *Le Globe*. Socialist tendencies are evident in the programme of the Spenceans who were active agitators in the London area in the period 1816–20, and, in a more elaborate form, in the work of William Thompson, John Minter Morgan, John Francis Bray and, of course, Robert Owen. In France, Louis Blanc, who unlike Owen made popular sovereignty the basis for his state socialism, published his *The Organisation of Labour* (1839), an influential tract in which he argued that the socialist government, elected by universal suffrage, should be constituted the supreme director of production and should divide profits between wages, support for the sick and aged, assistance to industries in temporary difficulties, and, finally, investment for expansion. Blanc, whose central passion was the co-operative social workshop under state patronage, was prepared to concede a limited sector of the economy to private enterprise.

Differing more on political than on economic grounds from state socialism was the collectivist doctrine advocated by Bakunin and many of his anarchist contemporaries. Like Proudhon, he thought in terms of local, federated production units, but with Bakunin the group of workers, the collectivity, took the place of the individual as the basic social unit. Bakunin accepted 'association,' Proudhon rejected it. Both were hostile to communism and to the formula, 'from each according to his abilities, to each according to his needs.' This formula provides a basic line of demarcation between collectivists and state socialists on the one hand and communists on the other (although there were exceptions: Thompson and Blanc both hoped, as socialists, that men would be rewarded on the basis of needs rather than of productivity).

Babeuf, the first of the modern communists, like Marx and Kropotkin after him, was in favour of 'needs.' But Babeuf's communism differed from that of his successors on two main counts: it envisaged the continued existence of the state; and it was distributive in emphasis rather than both productive and distributive. In other words, although all property must belong to the community, the peasant could borrow and farm a lot of his own, bringing the produce to the communal store where it would be distributed among the local population on the basis of needs. Babeuf's imagination was restricted by the pre-industrial society in which he lived; Marx and Kropotkin, aware of the technical advantages of large-scale farming, naturally insisted that the communist principle must extend to the sphere of production as well as distribution.

Kropotkin, who abhorred the state (and with it Babeuf), became the leading exponent of anarchist communism, which the anarchist Federation of the Jura adopted in 1880 in place of Bakuninist collectivism. Wherein exactly lay the difference? The collectivists were not convinced that men would work without incentives; Kropotkin answered, not altogether convincingly, that American slave owners and Russian serf owners resisting emancipation had asked the same question. But this analogy had obvious defects. The collectivists' solution was to issue work tickets for a day's labour, although they were divided as to whether skilled labour merited

Russian serfs on the Don, early nineteenth century.
Serfdom was not abolished until 1861. Even then, the freed
peasants laboured under heavy redemption payments.
Their plight inspired the Populist movement of the 1860's and 1870's.
Despite their sufferings, the majority of peasants remained loyal
to the Tsar and his church and did not respond to revolutionary agitation.

more tickets than unskilled. In Kropotkin's eyes this was no solution at all, merely a substitute for money wages and therefore a relic
of the capitalist mentality. He, like Proudhon, could find no viable
criterion for differentiating between the different services that men
rendered to society, no way of comparing the contribution of the
miner, who risked his life, with that of the engineer, who had
developed a specialised skill. He was convinced that science, if
properly harnessed and adapted to social needs, would create a
world of abundance, ensuring that working hours were both
pleasant and brief. In which case why make work obligatory?

The feature which distinguished Marxism from the alternative
formulas advocated within the economic Left was its historical
approach. Marx's rivals said: capitalism is unjust and irrational;
state socialism/communism or libertarian mutualism/collectivism/

communism, as the case might be, is the only just and workable system and ought to be introduced as soon as possible. Marx substituted dialectical evolution for the moral imperative. He argued that economic systems, feudal, capitalist, state socialist, communist, succeeded one another in logical succession and were determined by mechanical factors such as technological progress, the accumulation of capital, the concentration of small productive units into large, progressive pauperisation, and so forth. Certainly the workers fought for socialism in order to gain a fair deal, but this impulse was only an important component in the dialectical motor, the subjective agent and reflection of an objective process. The workers would build socialism *because they must*; their freedom was determined by necessity.

About the actual organisation of socialism Marx said very little and about communism even less. His life's work was devoted to examining the workings of capitalism and to demonstrating how it must inevitably lead to its own negation, to socialism. Nevertheless, certain points are clear. He regarded nationalisation as basic to the construction of socialism; he was committed to planning, although he said nothing about how to plan; he was sure that in suppressing itself (i.e. its own status) through socialism, the proletariat would suppress all classes.

The present chapter is concerned mainly with theories; a later one will approach the attempts to put these theories into practice. But it is perhaps relevant to note at this juncture that no actual society has so far incarnated any single and unadulterated theory. Almost everywhere rewards are based on both productivity and needs; only the emphasis varies. In the twentieth century, the economic Left has veered either towards 'managerial socialism,' as the reformists have tended to do, or towards state socialism, as the communists have, or, thirdly, towards the co-operative system, the most left-wing variant being that in which the workers themselves control a publicly owned co-operative. Spanish anarcho-syndicalism expressed this aspiration in its pure form, while Yugoslav communism has so far settled for a modified form.

9 The labour unions

More often than not the European manual worker had regarded his labour union as an organisation of more immediately personal importance than his political party. For one thing, the unions, as custodians of the worker's daily interests, contrast with the more remote and theoretical aims of the party; for another, politicians are suspect. In the nineteenth century the European unions were by no means invariably left-wing: the Italian Workers' Associations, which Mazzini strove to convert, regarded political questions as irrelevant to their sectional interests; the German Hirsch-Duncker Trade Associations preached an active collaboration between capital and labour; and the skilled craft unions of mid-Victorian Britain were committed to the Liberal Party.

But in modern Europe such instances are exceptional, and the vast majority of unions have inclined at least nominally to the Left. The diversity of forms which this orientation may take is practically limitless, but European experience suggests three principal models: the democratic-reformist, either more or less subordinated to the Socialist or Labour Party; the revolutionary syndicalist, entirely opposed to all political parties; and the communist, completely subordinated to the Communist Party. Each of these models will be examined briefly.

The dock strike of 1889, in London. From a contemporary print sold by street hawkers. In this strike the leadership of genuine socialists made itself felt. The labour movement was fast breaking away from the Liberal Party.

The democratic-reformist unions

Historically, the home not only of the democratic-reformist union but of the labour union itself was Britain. After twenty-six years of prohibition, an Act of 1825 legalised the unions, permitting workers to combine for collective bargaining and to embark on strike action. Many of the early union leaders were Owenite socialists or advocates of democratic parliamentary reform. When the Reform Bill dashed the hopes of the democrats, the National Union of the Working Classes, which preached both socialism and class struggle, concepts which had hitherto generally been kept separate, fell back on a militant syndicalism, on industrial action for political ends. The Chartist movement, however, encouraged a return to the more familiar practice of negotiation and strike action for short-term economic advantages, while to some extent succeeding in incorporating the unions in the wider campaign for political democracy.

With the defeat of Chartism and the onset of a long period of prosperity the unions, particularly the skilled craft unions, broke with the Left and began to concentrate on immediate economic advantages, on what Lenin called 'negative trade-unionism.' Despite the passions aroused by the American Civil War and despite the enthusiastic support given to the First International by George Odger, Henry Broadhurst and other union leaders, the large majority of the members of the Trades Union Congress were, at the time of its foundation in 1868, still hostile to any plan for an independent Labour Party. The TUC Parliamentary Commission preferred to act as a pressure group, as what Engels disparagingly but not unjustly called a 'tail of the great Liberal Party'. A safe, if imperfect, reality, a 'going concern', seemed preferable to a venture into idealism, to a precarious and costly adventure.

But the Liberals were exasperatingly slow in meeting the demands of labour, and in the late 1880's socialist doctrines at last began to percolate through to some members of the union rank and file. In the great dock strike of 1889 the dockers found in Tom Mann and John Burns socialist leaders of real ability and devotion. The newer unions, which absorbed and organised unskilled labour with little to lose in a direct political struggle, were the dynamic force in pulling the movement to the left and in providing a basis of mass support for the new Labour Party at whose annual Conference they commanded a majority of votes.

By the early 1920's, it was clear beyond doubt that the general influence of the unions was to act as a brake on revolutionary or genuinely socialist programmes. The apparent swing to the left in 1924–5, when the Bolshevik union leader Tomsky was twice invited to Britain amidst a wave of violent resolutions, was belied by the outcome of the general strike in 1926. The strike, initially an act of solidarity with the miners, who were threatened with redundancy and wage-cuts, but in reality a protest against the blind egoism of the Tory government and the City of London, was denounced by the Baldwin government as political and therefore unconstitutional. The union leaders, far from meeting the challenge, hastened to explain that it was an industrial strike alone. On 12 May the TUC leaders capitulated unconditionally without having gained any real assurances on behalf of the miners who fought on until surrender became unavoidable in November. The ten-day strike had cost the Transport and General Workers' Union, to take one

example, £600,000, £100,000 more than its annual revenue. Never again did the British unions attempt to exercise pressure on the government of the day by *general* industrial action.

In Germany as in Britain, the unions have tended to conform to the democratic-reformist model and to be unaffected by syndicalism, although the communist element after 1918 was more considerable. After the repeal of the Anti-Socialist Laws in 1890, the unions outdistanced the Party in the headlong gallop towards reformism and bureaucratisation, although their cautious empiricism kept them out of the 'revisionist' controversy. But what they lost in idealism they gained in efficiency. Whereas the British unions tended to represent a multitude of separate trades and crafts and jealously guarded their autonomy (there were perhaps 1,100 unions in 1914), the Germans constructed centralised industrial unions of which there were only fifty-one in 1911. This system enabled the centralised control of strike funds and their deployment with devastating effect in a selected local conflict. In contrast, the British unions lacked the discipline, cohesion and financial resources necessary for modern industrial warfare.

The German 'free' unions grew to maturity in the 1870's under socialist guidance and as part of a co-ordinated national movement. The common assumption that they enjoyed less independence from political interference than their British counterparts, that they were the sons rather than the father of a political party, is only partially true and certainly does not apply after 1900. The Mannheim Agreement of 1906 which ratified the equal status of the unions and the SPD reflected the real balance of power. In 1905 the Party had endorsed the principle of the general strike as a revolutionary weapon, but the resolution evaporated into hot air when in the same year the unions denounced all political general strikes, whether aimed at political reforms, anti-militarist, or intended to overthrow the existing social order. (The most common type of general strike in pre-1914 Europe was the political-reformist, of which there were instances in Belgium in 1893, Catalonia and Sweden in 1902, the Netherlands in 1903, Italy in 1904, and Sweden again in 1909. In 1913 the Belgian unions succeeded in procuring manhood suffrage by this strategy.) On one occasion, however, the German reformist unions resorted to the political general strike and with complete success. In 1920, the Federation of Labour under the leadership of the veteran Karl Legien, staged a nationwide strike to paralyse the Kapp-Luttwitz militarist *putsch*. The strike call was almost everywhere obeyed and the *putsch* failed.

The Swedish general strike of 1909 to which we have referred was defeated by the consolidated power of the large capitalist concerns. Yet the Swedish Workers' Confederation, the LO, provides the most notable example of a successful and far-sighted democratic-reformist labour movement. The LO, founded in 1898 and with 553,000 members by 1930, comprised in its finally evolved form forty-six federations of industrial and local unions, each federation having the capacity to sign collective agreements, decide on strike measures and generally supervise professional conditions. Embracing ninety per cent of Sweden's unionised workers by 1946, the LO had been responsible for the law of 1916 on accidents, the law of 1929 on sickness and the law of 1934 on insurance and

German General Strike, 1920.
There was heavy street fighting in Berlin.
Here workers are seen being taken under
arrest by soldiers supporting the right-wing Kapp *putsch*.
It was against this *putsch* that Kark Legien called for a nationwide strike.
The strike worked well and Kapp gave up.

employment, besides much other welfare legislation. The Social Democratic Party's remarkable political record has undoubtedly been a key factor in enabling the unions to adopt a constructive attitude and to avoid the sectarian obstructionism which becomes inevitable under a hostile régime.

In France, Italy and Spain the unions have conformed to the democratic-reformist model less consistently than in northern Europe. The French workers' associations which adhered to the First International were generally mutualist in the tradition of Proudhon and as such hostile to the state and political parties. After 1892 the more militant unions were syndicalist and after 1945 they were communist-dominated; only in the inter-war years did democratic reformism gain anything resembling supremacy.

British unemployed marching along
the London embankment, March 1930.
The second Labour government was in office.
The world economic crisis eventually
benefited the Right in Britain and Germany,
the Left in France and Sweden.

After 1918 white-collar workers and civil servants swelled the ranks of the CGT, swamping the veteran syndicalist militants and demanding the nationalisation of key industries and social insurance, thereby discarding the syndicalist rejection of the state in all its forms. Although the CGT merged with the communist CGTU in 1936 in support of the Popular Front policy of unity on the Left, the reformist wing led by Léon Jouhaux (who when elected General Secretary in 1909 had been a libertarian syndicalist) broke away in 1947 and formed *Force Ouvrière*, a small confederation of unions supported by the more reformist civil servants, white-collar and railway workers, closely aligned to the Socialist Party, and initially

May Day (1923) demonstration by members of the
Printers' Union in Stockholm. The Swedish labour movement
was now beginning to make its weight felt.
The first Social Democrat government had taken office in 1920.
After the Second World War, the Social Democrats became
the governing party in Sweden.

sustained both morally and financially by the American Federation
of Labor – a spearhead in the war against communism.

Less systematically hostile to political parties than the French,
the Italian unions entered their heroic phase immediately after
the First World War. Closely allied to the Socialist Party, the CGL
displayed the same combination of revolutionary ardour and ultimate caution. In January 1919 the CGL called for a republic, the
abolition of the Senate, proportional representation and the control
of foreign affairs by the Chamber of Deputies – a bold affirmation
of the right of unions to intervene in every sphere of politics. In
July, the CGL staunchly supported the international general strike

FRANCE

against the Allied intervention in Russia; and in August 1920 the Federation of Metal Workers gave the order for the occupation of the factories in the North. The situation was plainly revolutionary, but reformist inhibitions and an innate caution held the CGL back from calling for an extension of the factory occupation into a socialist seizure of power. As a result the CGL, like the Socialist Party itself, split, losing a minority of over one-quarter to the new Communist Party. Where the German unions succeeded in checking the counter-revolution in 1920, the Italians failed in 1922. The anti-fascist strike of August 1922 was badly prepared and merely provided a pretext for harsh repressive measures.

If the CGL had its quasi-revolutionary moments, less obviously 'quasi' was the spirit of the Spanish *Unión General de Trabajadores*

(UGT), established in 1888 in unrewarding conditions by Pablo
Iglesias, who also founded the Socialist Party itself. The UGT,
which by 1931 had almost 1,000,000 members, concentrated mainly
in Castile, but which was always overshadowed in Catalonia by the
anarcho-syndicalist CNT, reflected at the time of the Civil War the
schism within the Party between Largo Caballero's revolutionary
left wing and the reformist element headed by Indalecio Prieto. In
some instances the UGT collaborated with the anarchists in setting
up collectives, while elsewhere it was instrumental in imposing the
conservative economic policy favoured by the communists.

Revolutionary syndicalism

It was in Spain and France that there developed the purest examples
of the second model to which we have referred, the revolutionary
syndicalist. The incidence of anti-state feeling in the French Left is
harder to explain satisfactorily than in the Spanish. For all but brief
periods of its development the Spanish state seemed inpenetrable
and beyond reform; also the federal aspect of syndicalism appealed
to the Catalonian workers who shared with the upper classes the
desire to break free from Castilian domination; for them, the
'state' was Madrid. The French Left, on the other hand, led Europe
in the art of either capturing the state or forcing it to reform; all
adult males had the vote after 1870 and the electoral machinery
was immeasurably less corrupt than in Spain. The answer would
appear to lie with a number of factors; doctrinal influences,
particularly Proudhon's; the fact that production units in France
remained on the whole smaller than in Britain or Germany, weak-
ening the cohesive bargaining power of the unions; and the
attitude of the state itself which did not concede full legality and
freedom of action to the unions until 1884.

The revolutionary syndicalist movement which rapidly expanded
in the 1890's had been foreshadowed not so much by the mutualists
of the Second Empire as by the collectivist syndicalism which,

under the leadership of Eugène Varlin, a martyr of the Commune, took root in Paris, Rouen, Lyons and Marseilles and fostered a number of strikes in 1869–70. But this current cannot be said to have attained the status of a powerful national movement until the foundation in 1895 of the *Confédération Général du Travail* on the basis of a hard-won collaboration between the Bourses and the Syndicats. The Bourses du Travail, which united the unions of a single town or district and which were therefore based on regional rather than on trade or industrial cohesion, were often more combative than the Syndicats, or trade unions. It was the Bourses which emphasised the solidarity of proletarians as proletarians; it was they which organised libraries, professional courses, a medical service and industrial research. Their great organiser and theorist, Fernand Pelloutier, who regarded them as forming the nuclei of the future collectivist, stateless society, had himself passed from radicalism to Marxism and finally to anarchism.

Numerically, the CGT was never strong. It represented no more than fifty per cent of union members and only about ten per cent of the industrial male population. But what it lacked in size it atoned for in vigour. In brief, the CGT was distinguished by four qualities; hostility to the state and political parties; sensitivity to any sign of internal bureaucratisation; a revolutionary spirit; and devotion to socialism, or collectivism.

We have already suggested some of the more general and constant factors which may help to account for anti-state feeling within the French Left. But the sharp growth of anti-parliamentarianism among the workers and their leaders in the period 1890–1906 demands a more localised explanation. Georges Sorel, an intriguing theorist, but one whose influence was confined almost exclusively to Italian syndicalist circles, suggested a feasible answer when he expressed disgust at the corruption of socialist deputies and the careerist exploitation of the Dreyfus affair by certain republican politicians. Nothing, he said, so much resembles a representative of the bourgeoisie as a representative of the proletariat. This was a widespread feeling among the workers themselves. The CGT pro-

Certificate of membership of the British Amalgamated Society of Engineers, Machinists, Millwrights, Smiths and Pattern Makers, showing a warm regard for religion, history, inventors and social harmony. The unions which represented the working-class 'aristocracy' jealously restricted their numbers and only cautiously discarded their particularist outlook.

claimed its complete independence of all political parties in the Amiens Charter of 1906. The revolutionaries carried the day against the reformists and those who favoured purely economic action.

Convinced that power corrupts, the syndicalists attempted to eradicate from their ranks any trace of bureaucracy. In 1911 there was one union official for every thousand metal workers in Germany; in France there was one for every 7,000. (The Spanish CNT also elected very few officials, and those for a term of one year only, at a worker's wage.) Yet syndicalism, which shared with anarchism the self-congratulatory vision of itself as composed of a militant élite, was inclined in practice to substitute a hierarchy of merit for a hierarchy of office. In terms of class consciousness and political aggression, the syndicalists could not but be aware of the superiority of the urban to the rural worker, of the skilled to the unskilled (who were apt to shrink from a show-down with the employers on account of their more precarious economic position), and, finally, of the really active minority within the ranks of skilled workers to the rest. The élite jealously guarded its dominance. Sorel exalted 'spontaneous' strikes but in reality the CGT knew that a general strike must be carefully controlled and co-ordinated.

The CGT was revolutionary. Militancy increased sharply in the years 1904–6 and victimisation by employers became more common. Victor Griffuelhes, who incarnated the period of intransigent militancy which began to wane after 1909, declared: 'the CGT is permanent illegality. The Party is not revolutionary. Universal suffrage is not worth a general strike.' Sorel exalted violence, pure social struggle, the power of 'myths' whereby the proletariat might release its energies, and he envisaged the passage from capitalism to socialism as an upheaval of indescribable violence. If in France the daily reality was less metaphysical and more pragmatic, among the Italian syndicalists his almost fascistic anti-rationalism and worship of violence as a necessary moral force found many disciples.

For a brief period the CGT was as good as its word, but in meeting the trials of strength and nerve which it launched, the Clemenceau and Briand governments belied Sorel's assertion that the bourgeoisie had become timid and vacillating. In April 1906 Clemenceau sent troops to the Pas de Calais, where the miners had stopped work, and declared a state of siege. In March 1907 troops clashed with strikers at Nantes, and in the same month troops helped to restore the electricity service in Paris. In the following year they fired on strikers at Draveil; when Clemenceau praised their action the CGT proclaimed a twenty-four hour general strike which resulted in another day of bloodshed and yet another strike. Strikes and government reprisals followed one another in rapid succession as anarchist terrorist outrages and official executions had in the 1890's. Clemenceau broke a strike of postal workers by dismissing the activists who were technically civil servants. Briand further developed this strategy in 1910 when he smashed a railway strike by employing troops and by calling up the railwaymen themselves into the army. Syndicalism in France had met its match in the shape of a determined and hostile state.

Lastly, the syndicalists were committed socialists, or collectivists, committed to the overthrow of capitalism. The unions, particularly the Bourses, were regarded as the organs of social regeneration, the basic units of socialist production to be administered by workers educated within the workshop ethos, who had learned to synthesise theoretical and practical experience, to overcome the barrier between physical and mental labour, and who understood the relation of the parts of the production system to the whole.

The Spanish CNT, as will be seen in a later chapter, made a valiant effort to realise these ideals in 1936–7. Syndicalism in Spain matured late; before 1914 it lacked the cohesion and self-confidence of its French counterpart; the CNT, which was founded in 1910, was in fact modelled on the CGT. By 1919 Salvador Seguí had fashioned a fighting force out of its 700,000 members and a war of the *pistoleros* raged in Barcelona until the La Cierva government sent in troops and banned the unions. In May 1924 the CNT was forcibly dissolved and almost ceased to exist until 1930, after which, with a strength of 1,500,000, it returned with new zeal to the tactics of strikes, boycotts, sabotage and armed resistance, tactics

which were transformed into a constructive strategy after the outbreak of the Civil War.

It was in fact the CNT alone which held the syndicalist banner high in the period between the two World Wars. After 1917 the European movement suffered a two-pronged attack from communism, at that moment evidently the only revolutionary creed able to live up to its ideals, and reformism, promising practical advantages in place of utopian ideals. Time-honoured inhibitions withered away. Griffuelhes, who visited Russia in 1920, managed to convince himself that the Bolshevik state was provisional and that the soviets provided the basis for a sound, de-centralised federalism. Jouhaux and the reformists pointed out that Bolshevism

Above: May 1937, in Paris. A trade union procession. The carnival atmosphere is balanced by the intent expressions of the marchers seen in the bottom left-hand corner.
Below: March 1963, during the miners' strike, metal workers of the communist CGT and of the Christian CFTC join in a demonstration at Merlebach in Lorraine.

151

represented all that syndicalism had opposed; yet they themselves had abandoned the revolutionary ideal during the war and during the strike waves of 1919–20 and their words consequently carried little conviction for the revolutionaries. Certainly the formal subordination of the Profintern – the communist international of labour unions – to the Comintern disturbed many a syndicalist conscience, but a dynamic force was hard to resist and in 1922 the break-away CGTU joined the Profintern without conditions. The syndicalists were soon disillusioned and departed into a lonely and unrewarding isolation. The CNT and the Italian syndicalists also learned of their error in 1922, broke with the Profintern and formed a new syndicalist International Workingmen's Association in Berlin. Now for the first time the three basic models coalesced into three rival Internationals; at Amsterdam, the democratic reformist; at Moscow, the communist; at Berlin, the syndicalist.

The communist unions

Marx was never inclined to ignore the labour unions; indeed the hard-core of the First International was comprised of French and British trade unionists. It was Marx's aim to persuade the unions to adopt a broad, political perspective over and beyond the day-by-day economic struggles which were their immediate *raison d'être*. Lenin later developed this position, criticising what he called 'economism,' an undue concentration on industrial disputes and on the betterment of the present generation rather than on the salvation of the next. Lenin proclaimed the absolute supremacy of the Party, at the same time urging communists to work within the unions and to combat reformism at every level. The unions were useful tools, nothing more. The second (1920) Congress of the Comintern laid down categorically that, 'the work . . . in the . . . industrial unions ought to be invariably and systematically directed by the Party of the proletariat, . . . the Communist Party.'

From the outset west European communists treated the unions as agencies for extending the Party's influence among the broad base of the industrial workers. Partly for this reason their influence in the British, French and German unions did not match that of the socialists; at the Leipzig Convention in 1922, for example, only ninety out of 694 delegates were communists. The sectarian policy which applied after 1928 to the Comintern and Profintern alike further divorced the communists from the mainstream of unionism, and it was not until the era of the united and popular fronts that they began to make up lost ground and to benefit from their ability to exercise a dual influence in a single enterprise, firstly through a trade union faction under their control, and, secondly, through the Party cells in the factory. The communists displayed an almost ubiquitous genius for organisation and discipline, for tagging the unions to the tail of a political manoeuvre.

After the war the communists captured control of the most important element of the French union movement, the CGT, urging wage restraint and higher productivity on the workers during their years in the government and then, after 1947, jettisoning all restraint and championing a wave of strikes. In Italy the *Confederazione generale italiana del Lavoro* (CGIL) followed a parallel course. Although the CGT had by 1950 fallen to one-quarter of its 1946 strength, it has remained the largest and most militant of the French union confederations, probably containing more socialists than *Force Ouvrière* and more Catholics than the *Confédération française des Travailleurs Chrétiens* (CFTC). The events of 1956 dealt a bad blow to the communist unions in France and an almost mortal one to those in Britain. The CGT, which lost twenty per cent of its vote in some thirty elections of shop stewards and plant committees, had to permit its departmental federations to express their own opinions on the Hungarian revolution, an event which induced a number of leading British trade unionists to resign from the Communist Party. No sooner had the Party begun to recover than it received another blow when certain of its members were convicted of ballot-rigging in the Electrical Trades Union. In Britain even communists are expected to heed the rules of 'fair play.'

PART THREE

The balance sheet

Above: End of the Robespierrists. The night of 27–28 July 1794.
Robespierre failed in a suicide attempt and was guillotined the next day.
Below: Vienna, October 1848, defeat of the revolutionaries. The monarchist
General Windischgraetz brings in Croatian peasant soldiers to crush them.

10 The anatomy of revolution

The revolutionary situation

There is the revolutionary situation and the revolutionary policy. This distinction, however useful for analysis, should not obscure their obvious interdependence, the fact that the Subject, the revolutionary, in attempting to master and mould the Object, the situation, is himself changed. A hot summer day is a static situation, beyond human control; a revolutionary crisis is a dynamic one, a reflection of human activity.

The event which sparks off a revolution is often not only trivial but also only incidentally relevant to the deeper sources of social tension which alone can transform a series of grievances into a revolutionary pattern. The economic factor is generally fundamental. Although poverty and unemployment may not in themselves be sufficient to generate a revolution, they constitute its most important element in nine cases out of ten. By June 1790, 31,000 unemployed had taken refuge in the workshops of Paris, and throughout the revolutionary period, 1789–94, the ratio of wages to prices – the cost of living – was a course of constant popular ferment. Indeed, the Champ de Mars demonstration of July 1791 stands out as the only great political *journée* in no way connected with the price of bread and other basic commodities.

What counts in this respect is not the absolute standard of living but relative decline; were this not the case, Afro-Asia would be in a state of constant revolution and Europe eternally placid. This relativity has to be considered from two aspects; the worker's real wage today as compared with yesterday, and the working-class share of the total national wealth today as compared with yesterday. During the French revolution the first aspect was more relevant, whereas Chartist violence issued more from the second, but generally the two go hand in hand since in any economic crisis the working class will tend to suffer more than the upper classes both absolutely and relatively. The revolutions of 1848 followed an acute depression which coincided with the last of the major European famines. About one-tenth of the population of Berlin had by 1846 resorted to crime or prostitution, while in

156

The Berlin revolution of 1918–19,
led by soldiers, sailors and local workers.
Having brought down the Kaiser and
introduced a parliamentary democracy, the
revolution became internally divided and failed
to progress further.

France 1847 was *l'année du pain cher*. The revolutions of 1905 and 1917–19 were foreshadowed by a progressive economic deterioration resulting from war damage, loss of productivity, heavy taxation, insolvency and inflation.

Hence the triviality and merely incidental relevance of the sparks which ignite the dry timber but of which the popular histories are inclined to make so much. The Parisians were outraged by the King's dismissal of Necker and, later, by his flight to Varennes. In 1848 the government's attempt to ban a reform banquet precipitated the fall of the monarchy; in 1905 the Bloody Sunday massacre inflamed the Russian people, and in January 1919 the communists rose in protest against the dismissal of a left-wing chief of police in Berlin. All this is true, but it is also trivial. Comparable incidents occur frequently in non-revolutionary situations and so receive scant attention.

But an economic crisis need not in itself imply a revolutionary crisis. The vast majority of revolutionary situations have also been war situations. A war not only increases poverty and worsens the economic crisis, it also desanctifies the sacred, transforms dignitaries into incompetents, makes heroes of exiles, disintegrates organisation. France had been at war in 1740–8, 1756–63 and 1776–83, and had been the loser on all but the last occasion. The cumulative cost was excessive; the American war and its debt broke the monarchy. Prussia's victory over Louis Bonaparte in 1870 and the subsequent siege of Paris generated a series of revolutionary *coups* from the setting up of the Government of National Defence until the insurrection which ushered in the Commune itself. In 1905, Russia had suffered a crushing defeat at the hands of Japan, in 1917 at the hands of the Central Powers. It was in fact the German Foreign Ministry, supported by the Political Section of the General Staff, which arranged for Lenin's return to Russia from Switzerland – an asp let loose upon a dying body politic.

The most serious revolutionary movements of 1919 and 1920 took place in defeated nations, Hungary and Germany, and in an exhausted one, Italy. In defeat the morale and loyalty of the armed

forces, the last resort of kings, collapses. In 1905 the war had been
less prolonged and total, with the result that the revolution foundered on the rock of military loyalty. But in February 1917 the
bourgeois revolution in Russia triumphed when the garrison troops
were found to be unreliable and the Cossacks consequently lost their
nerve. By October the Bolsheviks were able to regard the garrison at
Petrograd as virtually their own. On 30 October the Hungarian regi-
ments mutinied and by the following day Budapest was in the hands
of a revolution which was later to derive much of its communistic
impetus from prisoners-of-war like Bela Kun who had been converted in Russia. On 7 November disaffected soldiers brought Kurt
Eisner's Soviet Republic to power in Bavaria, and two days later
the Kaiser abdicated when the hostility of the Berlin garrison and
of the workers' and soldiers' councils seemed to leave him no
alternative.

War is negation; as such it favours the destructive revolution.
But war transformed becomes affirmation; as such it binds together
the constructive revolution. The dynamic of the Jacobin revolution gathered strength with the war of 1792 and with the ability of

Bela Kun, leader of the short-lived communist régime in Hungary, in 1919. Kun later worked for the Comintern and disappeared in the Stalinist purges of 1936–8.

Jacobinism to identify itself with patriotism and its opponents with national treason. Later, the Bolsheviks donned the same mantle in the civil war against the White generals and the Allies. It goes without saying that such wars only bind the revolution if victorious, and that they have not always been so. The Hungarian revolution of 1848–9 was crushed by a Russian army. In 1871 the war against Prussia was already over and the Communards lost rather than gained support among the majority of Frenchmen by their threat to revive it. Bela Kun's war with Rumania in 1919 proved the ruin of his régime.

If the revolution may at any stage succumb to superior external force, so it is no less true that the revolutionary (particularly if he is an extremist whose moment may arrive rather late in the proceedings) cannot rely on the internal forces of the state withering away mechanically. Time and again revolutions have come up against a situation, an adverse balance of forces, which it was beyond their power to redress, and so have foundered. The Babouvists looked hopefully to the mutinous *Légion de Police* at Grenelle, but they quickly discovered how easily a single Legion could be disbanded by the loyal forces of the state. Vienna fell in October 1848 to the Hapsburg army commanded by Windischgraetz, a regular army strong enough to overcome the forces of the revolution, the National Guard, the University Legion and the militia. Throughout Europe in 1848–9 it was their control of the army which enabled the conservatives to retain their ultimate preponderance and to force the revolutionaries into a submission they could do little to avert. Thiers' government at Versailles had by April 1871 gathered an army which, if no match for the Prussians, had the capacity to drown the Paris Commune in blood.

In Berlin and Bavaria the communists were doomed in 1919 once the socialist Minister of the Interior, Gustave Noske, had found it in his heart to employ as agents of repression the counter-revolutionary, para-military units, the *Freikorps*. The Red rising in the Ruhr in 1920 was easily snuffed out by the army, the *Reichswehr*, acting under the orders of the socialist Chancellor Hermann Muller. Three years later the Russian and German communists worked in collaboration on an elaborate revolutionary plan which proved to be based on two false calculations; the degree of pro-communist sympathy among the regular police and army, and the ability of the 'Red Hundreds' in Saxony and Thuringia to transform themselves into a cohesive army of 60,000 workers which would march irresistibly on Berlin, sweeping all opposition aside. On 14 October President Ebert ordered General Adolf Muller to supplant the local left-wing governments in Saxony and Thuringia. Muller entered Dresden without difficulty; the revolution, confronted with the real balance of power, collapsed before it had begun. In the same way, the tragic war waged by the Asturian miners in 1934 against General Franco's regular Moorish divisions was from the outset a lost cause.

But these factors can be viewed in another light. Military power is, after all, primarily a manifestation of economic power and social dominance, and it is therefore not unreasonable to regard the balance of social forces as constituting the fundamental factor in any revolutionary situation. The Jacobins increasingly benefited from the support of a wide variety of occupational categories ranging from wine merchants to wage earners who gradually achieved a subjective harmony, almost a cohesive class consciousness, and who provided the horse-power for each revolutionary advance. The Jacobins rode a horse composed of these *sans-culottes* and of important elements of the lower middle class and peasantry. Ultimately, however, the horse fell apart. Once isolated from the masses, once unable to resolve the contradictory movements of its discordant limbs, the 'petitbourgeois' Jacobins fell an easy prey to the conservative and pro-Girondin bourgeoisie. The reaction of Thermidor which sent Robespierre and his colleagues to the guillotine drew barely a murmur from the faubourgs of Paris.

The French revolution of 1848 lost its social cohesion more rapidly. As Marx said, 'in common with the bourgeoisie, the workers made the February revolution . . .'. But, as de Tocqueville testified, fear seized the middle classes as it had never done after 1789; fear, like sin, needs a precedent; the riotous *sans-culottes*, like Adam and Eve, represented to later generations an original sin which was unforgettable. The moderate republicans had from the outset a seven-to-four majority in the Provisional Government which was determined to curb the Parisian extremists who, unlike their predecessors of 1792–4, were unable to harness the support of sympathetic groups in the provinces. When in June the frustrated proletarians of Paris rose in desperation, the middle classes crushed them with exemplary savagery. In Germany, equality before the law, a national parliament and an extension of the franchise sufficed to satisfy the bourgeoisie who hastily organised civic guards to curb the lower orders should they mistake the revolution for their own. In Wurttemberg and Hanover the workers were declared ineligible to vote and in Bavaria only taxpayers were granted the franchise. The conservative junkers observed the revolution dissolve in fratricidal social struggle and bided their time. In 1848, moreover, the negative attitude of the peasantry everywhere tipped the social balance in favour of the counter-revolution. Whereas in 1789 the peasant risings had undermined the quasi-feudal state and prevented the old régime from holding out against the frontal attack of the towns, the revolutions of 1848 were weakened by their exclusively urban character. The Austrian Alpine provinces made no attempt to aid revolutionary Vienna. The peasants of Central Europe, once relieved of their feudal obligations, became fanatics of 'order,' the raw material of the armies of repression. Proudhon reminds us how the French peasants welcomed the blood-letting of the 'June days' in Paris.

No factor did more to cripple the Paris Commune than its social isolation, an isolation attested by the fact that in the National Assembly elected in February 1871 the Jacobin and socialist Left could claim only twenty out of 630 seats. On 18 March a Central Committee manifesto issued in Paris denounced 'the failures and treasons of the ruling classes,' and warned that the Parisian proletariat had decided to save the situation 'by taking into their own hands the direction of public affairs . . .' The 'decent folk' were not enchanted by this frankness and the rural masses, including the landless labourers, found no difficulty in swallowing the propaganda issuing from Versailles and in believing, like Taine, that the Communard leaders were 'fanatics, cosmopolitan strangers, rogues who risk everything in order to create a new *jacquerie*.' In 1905 the objectively revolutionary classes in Russia knew one another little. The grudging and patently insincere concessions made by the Tsar were enough to split the bourgeoisie, many of whom preferred on reflection the autocracy to the awakening of the primeval masses. The peasants were in a violent mood but they failed to correlate their grievances with a revolutionary ideology and to develop a sense of solidarity with the urban workers. The same proved true in Germany in 1919; the Soviet Republic in Bavaria failed to awaken real sympathy in either the peasantry or the middle classes who were now haunted by Bolshevism as in 1848 they had been haunted by memories of the Terror. Bela Kun's régime lost no time in alienating the Hungarian peasantry by nationalising the land rather than redistributing it.

The year of the two Russian revolutions.
A crowd gathered in the square before the Winter Palace, Petrograd 1917.
The many soldiers seen in the picture illustrate the cardinal
importance for the Bolsheviks of winning over the
Petrograd garrison to their side.
In October, they stormed the Winter Palace.

   The Bolsheviks on the other hand were blessed by a peasantry
whose traditional conservatism and susceptibility to clerical influence had been finally eradicated by desperate poverty and who
were willing to support any party or class which would champion
them against the landlords and so assuage their land hunger. The
middle classes were not so much friendly towards the workers as
demoralised and lacking the historical tradition of self-assertion
which would have enabled them to follow up their victory in
February by simultaneously fighting a war and creating a state
machine strong enough to keep the masses under control. With the
overthrow of the Kerensky government by the Bolsheviks, the
Russian middle classes disappeared from history as a political
force as humbly as they had arrived.

Revolutionary tactics

The fine line which divides the 'situation' from the 'tactics,' the response of the Object from the activities of the Subject, can be illustrated by a resumption of the discussion on the balance of power and military force in a slightly altered perspective. Certainly the revolution may encounter a situation where no amount of cunning and endeavour can compensate for the social and military superiority of its opponents. Yet the evidence suggests that an adverse or even apparently hopeless situation can sometimes be reversed with surprising rapidity by a class determined and confident of its ability to command the stage. The revolutionary bourgeoisie in France quickly implemented its decision to bring the Crown under control by forming its own National Guard whose officers swore to use their troops only under the orders of the municipal authorities. Later the National Guard defended the bourgeoisie with equal determination against the Left, against the *sans-culottes;* the massacre of the Champ de Mars in July 1791 served as a prelude to the arrest of left-wing politicians who were held to have insulted Lafayette and his Guard. But the Left, the Cordeliers Club and the Jacobins, gradually evolved an answer of their own by harnessing the eruptive power of the *sans-culottes* to their own chariot, by launching the popular battalions with devastating effect on selected political *journées*. With popular power in the ascendant, the Commune of Paris issued an order, on 11 July 1792, that all citizens who possessed pikes should be drafted into the National Guard; the character of the National Guard was abruptly transformed from bourgeois conservatism to democratic radicalism. A system was evolved whereby each of the forty-eight sections of Paris possessed its own National Guard battalion, whose movements and actions it could direct. The Commune enjoyed overall control of the Guard and of the police.

But the precedent was one which the extreme Left conspicuously failed to imitate in 1848. In June the proletarian insurrection could find no answer except a futile heroism against the volleys of the bourgeois National Guard. In Germany and Austria workers were

Trotsky crossing Red Square
on the occasion of the Red Army sports in October 1923.
A man of outstanding stature.
both as a leader and as a thinker,
Trotsky was soon to allow his position to be undermined by Stalin.
In 1940 he was murdered with an ice-axe in Mexico.

rigorously excluded from the National Guard, which in March was responsible for shooting or imprisoning thousands of workers in the Viennese suburbs and in August for the massacre at the 'Battle of the Prater.' On the eve of the Commune of 1871, in October 1870, the Guard had been as usual the final resort of a moderate Left government defending itself against a revolutionary *coup* launched by the extreme Left, by Blanqui, Flourens and the clubs. But the continuing isolation of Paris resulted in the workers, and later the unemployed, swelling the ranks of the Guard until its social composition and sympathies had been transformed out of all recognition. It offered no resistance to the rising of 18 March, and thereafter, under the Commune, it conducted the defence of revolutionary Paris against Thiers' army.

History (and technology) worked in favour of the state. Engels pointed out in 1895 how in the period since 1848 regular armies grew larger, railways appeared to facilitate the rapid reinforcement of garrisons, and the development of small-calibre, breech-loading magazine rifles and percussion shells strengthened the mailed fist of the *status quo*. Consequently – and this was a factor of cardinal importance – National Guards and civilian militias in general could no longer hope to hold out on their own against the regular forces of the state. Disaffection *within the regular army* became vital. In 1905 Trotsky and the St Petersburg Soviet waited in vain for some sign of support among the garrison troops; in December the Moscow workers fought without hope. Trotsky himself mocked the Russian bourgeoisie for failing to create a militia because, he said, it knew that to arm the revolution meant arming the workers, but the fact remains that no revolutionary militia could at that moment have triumphed against the regular army. Indeed the mutiny on the Battleship *Potemkin* and the mood of disaffection within the Black Sea Fleet was for the autocracy the most worrying incident of the whole year. In 1917 the Petrograd Soviet created a military-revolutionary committee which prepared for the seizure of power and a Red Guard of factory workers which was able to assume command of the city when the moment arrived, but the

success of the whole operation depended on the fact that the local garrison and naval units were impregnated with Bolshevism and that Kerensky could find no loyal unit to summon to his aid.

To emphasise the interdependence of the situation and the tactics is not, of course, to underestimate the importance of the quality of the revolutionary leadership. The successful revolution acts decisively. If circumstances are the mothers of revolutions, men themselves act as the midwives and miscarriages resulting from hesitation are not unknown. The successful revolution sheds blood; offered death, it chooses to live. But in doing so it faces a trap; beyond a certain point blood-letting becomes (moral factors apart) self-defeating. The Jacobins fought a civil war without quarter; the rebellious towns of Toulon and Lyons met with terrible punishments and with mass executions in December 1793. All the Girondin leaders who were put on trial were executed and those who, like Roland, Pétion, Buzot and Barbaroux, evaded the guillotine were hunted down and exterminated. In April 1794 Danton and thirteen colleagues, who hoped to reconcile the left and right wings within the Convention and who challenged Robespierre's policy of continued war and terror, were executed. During the fourteen months of Jacobin control of the Convention there were 17,000 official executions, a slaughter which became politically and socially increasingly indiscriminate during the period of unmitigated dictatorship from April till June 1794. Like all orgies, it was self-defeating; when one day it was Robespierre whose head fell, Parisians were too dazed to note what this might signify.

The Bolsheviks took this aspect of the Jacobin lesson to heart and moved, in the first instance, with extreme caution. The anarchists were the first to suffer in the Spring of 1918 when about 180 of their leading spirits were either imprisoned or liquidated, but the Left SR's, although responsible for an attempt on Lenin's life, were not immediately declared illegal. It was the Civil War which broke down restraint; it could not but do so. By 1921, twenty-six of the Left SR leaders had been shot. The Cheka was set up as an instrument of 'direct justice'; forced labour was introduced. When Trotsky, whose *Defence of Terrorism* (1920) revealed an existential will to dominate and regulate, decided for reasons of efficiency to incorporate former Tsarist officers in the Red Army, he insured their loyalty by the most simple of deterrents – the threat to execute their families in the event of desertion.

Revolutionary terror has almost invariably suffered both a quantitative and qualitative change for the worse. Not only is its dynamic self-perpetuating, but it tends to degenerate from mass terror into police terror, from the spontaneous act of popular assertion of September 1792, 1918 and July–September 1936 (in Spain) to the systematic strategy of extermination of 1794, 1936–8 (in Russia) and 1937–8 (in Spain). In a time of supreme danger suspects are cut down. Before departing for the front, the Parisians massacred priests, prisoners and prostitutes, actions not morally laudable or wholly rational but valid in so far as they were dictated by a cruel necessity. The Spanish working class lost no time in settling accounts with their enemies and included among their victims, tragically, hundreds of nuns, but, then as before, revolutionary justice assumed its own logic and the Church as a whole had unequivocally thrown its weight behind the upper classes and right-wing authoritarianism. But what follows is the gradual mutation of mass terror into a more calculated police terror, directed at first against the class enemy but later at all who do not share the faith of a single party or group or, as was the case under Stalin, of a single man.

In bourgeois mythology revolution is pure negation, purely

destructive, the work of 'subversives,' 'foreign agents,' Taine's 'cosmopolitan rogues.' In fact the successful revolution is constructive and optimistic; it does not imagine that its cause can triumph on the streets alone; it begins to examine existing institutions rationally in terms of their future possibilities. It confines its destructive blows to those spheres where constructive work may follow. Thus the Commune of Paris and the Jacobin Club, realising that the Legislative Assembly would never become an instrument of the Left, organised the insurrection of 10 August 1792 which resulted in its overthrow and in the election of the National Convention. Exerting steady internal pressure reinforced at calculated moments by violent external pressure, the Jacobins finally made the Convention their own; Marat and Robespierre were responsible for the insurrections of 31 May and 2 June 1793 when the Parisians invaded the Assembly and forced the arrest of twenty-nine Girondin leaders.

Lenin later codified these tactics and dismissed as 'infantile' any *a priori* insistence that existing institutions were beyond permeation and redemption. Each case had to be judged on its merits; the revolutionary in search of the appearance of legitimacy must fasten on whatever element of organic continuity he finds at his disposal. Soon after his return to Russia Lenin adopted the slogan, 'all power to the soviets! – to an existing institution. But when in June only 105 of the 822 delegates elected to the first All-Russian Congress of Soviets were found to be Bolsheviks, he quickly dropped the slogan, readopting it only after the abortive Kornilov *putsch* created a favourable climate of opinion in which the Bolsheviks were able to gain the upper hand in the Petrograd and Moscow soviets. Such strategy not only bestows on the revolutionary party the appearance of organic legitimacy, it also undermines the influence of the opposition and of rival parties.

But the revolution rapidly fashions its own instruments. The Committee of Public Safety, in its finally evolved, Robespierrist form, represented a hard, compact and flexible executive organ composed of deputies elected by the Convention and enjoying a

Hesitant, equivocating and a luke-warm socialist, Alexander Kerensky attempted to continue the war against Germany in the summer of 1917, after the fall of the Tsar. The attempt failed and in October the Bolsheviks capitalised on the situation to seize power. In one respect only did Kerensky have the last word; forty years after Lenin's death, twenty-four years after Trotsky's, and eleven years after Stalin's, he was still alive.

wide variety of powers; to veto ministerial measures and, subject to the approval of the Convention, to nominate generals, direct foreign policy and purge the local authorities. If the Committee of Public Safety never succeeded in making of the Convention a mere rubber stamp in the way that the Bolshevik executive, the Politburo, manipulated the soviets, the parallel – the emphasis on executive efficiency – is nevertheless an instructive one, particularly in the light of the failures of 1848. Far from creating an autonomous and all-powerful executive organ, the French republicans of that year committed, despite the warnings of Blanqui and others, the error of holding a general election. As a result, the Jacobins controlled only 100 of the 900 seats. Manhood suffrage never serves a revolution well. The Austrian workers, granted the vote after the famous Storm Petition of May 1848, failed to return a single deputy of their own to the Reichstag. Although the Paris Commune was a body elected by manhood suffrage, the vote was confined to Paris alone where the bourgeoisie was depleted and paralysed into abstention and where no peasant foot trod. Yet when the crisis became acute, as it invariably does, the elected Commune hastened to delegate its powers to a Committee of Public Safety. The Bolsheviks, finding themselves in a small minority within the National Constituent Assembly, decided in January 1918 to dispense with 'petty bourgeois democracy' and promptly terminated its existence.

Necessary though it is, this (institutional) synthesis of revolutionary negation and affirmation is of minor importance when set beside the larger economic and social problems which must immediately be resolved. The French revolution, in turning over considerable tracts of land to the middle classes and peasantry, was able simultaneously to cripple the counter-revolutionary class at the source of its power and to give the majority of the population a vested interest in its survival. The National Assembly abolished tithes, annates and clerical pluralism; it nationalised Church land and sold it off in plots for depreciated paper money. Later, crown lands and the holdings of *émigrés* were also put on the market.

Where Kerensky had appealed to the Russian peasants to wait patiently for legislative reform, Lenin's first action was to sanction the distribution of the great estates. Rosa Luxemburg was doubtless correct in prophesying that this action would impede the progress of socialism by strengthening the proprietorial (kulak) element among the peasants, but subsequent events belied her assertion that the peasant 'does not even dream of defending Russia and the revolution to which he owes his land.'

Nor can the unequivocal support of the urban workers be taken for granted indefinitely. The Jacobins succeeded at first in channelling the unemployed into the army and, by a policy of controls, in halting inflation and arresting for several months the fall in the value of the *assignat*. But in the long run the Administration failed to resolve the contradiction between the demands of the *sans-culottes* and the demands of the war effort. In this respect the Bolsheviks benefited from their overt commitment to the proletariat and by the rapidity with which they established the principle of the

The classic revolutionary scene.
A crowd dispersing under fire. Petrograd, 1917.

eight-hour day, the forty-eight hour week, social insurance for the unemployed and the sick, and the prohibition of child labour. This was naturally easier said than done, but the psychological effect was important in enabling Lenin to appeal to the constructive impulses of the workers.

The French and Russian revolutions played out the final drama of their birth – a war both civil and foreign – with a success which attested not only to the military genius of a Carnot and a Trotsky, to the administrative ability of a Robespierre and a Lenin, but also to the soundness of the social and economic policies which had rallied the popular masses to the revolutionary armies. The Jacobins performed a near-miracle; in June 1793, sixty out of eighty departments were in revolt against them, the German princes were invading from the North and East, the British were attacking from the South and West. Fourteen months later the revolt had been extinguished, the invaders expelled and Belgium occupied. And an army grown three-fold was being run on a budget cut by half. Early in 1919 the Bolsheviks were blockaded by sea, threatened by a Japanese army in Siberia, by British forces in the North and the French in the South, and destined to face a series of strong thrusts from the White generals, Kolchak, Wrangel, Denikin and Yudenich. Yet by the summer of 1920 the counter-revolution was defunct, the Allies had given up the struggle and a Red Army 5,000,000 strong had reached the 'gates' of Warsaw.

It would, however, be absurd to judge a revolution in terms of its ability to wage war. For the Left, war is only a means to an end; the final judgment lies in the realm of popular sovereignty.

Permanent revolution

A 'revolution' is an ambiguous entity. In any single 'revolution' there may in fact be one, two or several, each treading on the heels of the one before and kicking viciously at the one behind. The liberals once in power take a stand against the Left; the moderate Left in its turn seeks to curb the extreme Left and to freeze the revolution to its own advantage. This process and its often dour consequences are observable in one instance after another. Moreover: to define and trace this process of internal conflict is in a sense to return to and restate the evidence used earlier in connection with the social balance of forces in a revolutionary situation. Here again the fine line dividing the 'situation' from the 'tactics' is revealed. Regarding class conflict as endemic, as an immutable determining factor, we say that the workers in a particular situation were *doomed* by the hostility, say, of the petite-bourgeoisie. But, regarding political action in a less deterministic light, as open to alternatives, we attribute to the Jacobins the *responsibility* for turning against the extreme Left. Thus, in putting the same story in a different light, we come across one of the most basic contradictions in historical analysis.

The Jacobins did not repeal the *loi Le Chapelier*; rather they invoked it to imprison workers for illegal assembly, and in the winter and spring of 1793–4 they adopted the habit of breaking strikes by requisitioning labour. Having used it to their own advantage against the Girondins, the Jacobins turned on and mutilated the tradition of direct democracy emanating from the clubs and the Commune of Paris. The *Enragés* were forcibly put down; certain clubs were closed; and the Commune itself was purged of Hébertist influence after Hébert, Ronsin, Vincent and Momoro, the leaders of the Cordeliers Club who, on 2 March, had proclaimed the necessity of a new insurrection, and had begun to attack the Robespierrists as '*endormeurs*,' were guillotined on 24 March. In a sense, the 'reaction' dated not from the fall of Robespierre but rather from November 1793, when the Jacobins began to suppress the extreme Left in all its forms; in another sense it can be argued that the first revolutionary consideration was the war effort and that the Hébertist Commune, in defying the law and failing to tax the *sans-culottes*, was guilty of demagogic betrayal. Whichever view one adopts the fact remains that the Jacobins did suppress the extreme Left and that their action was motivated as much by class prejudice as by purely administrative considerations.

In 1848–9 the same pattern repeated itself. The Provisional Government showed an exaggerated respect for all forms of private property and set up the National Workshops without any intention of making them function in the way Louis Blanc had visualised. When on 16 April a demonstration took place in favour of raising the workers' wages and delaying the national elections, the neo-Jacobin Minister of the Interior, Ledru-Rollin, promptly called out the National Guard. A month later the extreme Left, led by Blanqui, Barbès and Raspail, invaded the new Constituent Assembly. The moderate Left thoroughly endorsed the reaction which ensued, the arrest of the leaders of the extreme Left, the closure of the National Workshops and General Cavaignac's ruthless suppression of the proletarian insurrection in June. On 13 June 1849 it was the turn of Ledru-Rollin and the officers of three legions of the Guard to demonstrate in the name of democracy and to be answered in the same language as the workers had been answered a year earlier. A revolution must drive forward or turn back; it cannot stand still.

More often than not the moderate Left will, in the event, choose to turn back. After the elections to the second Russian Duma in 1907, Miliukov, the leader of the democratic Cadets, commented: 'as to the left groups in the narrower sense of the word, that is the socialist and revolutionary groups, an agreement with them will be more difficult.' It was, indeed, impossible. In 1917 the Cadets and the Right SR's, the beneficiaries of the February revolution, once again attempted to check the extreme Left, but on this occasion without success. It is perhaps less obvious but not less true that the German majority socialists, in their anxiety to limit the revolution to its democratic phase by any means at their disposal, were responsible for the fatal weakness of the Weimar Republic.

Finally, how in this perspective are we to judge the record of the Bolshevik revolution? To say that it was the second revolution, that it superseded the bourgeois revolution, that the Bolsheviks represented the extreme Left, is not to solve the problem. Within a few months Lenin was confronted by sharp criticism from the Left Communists and Left SR's over the Treaty of Brest-Litovsk and the question of egalitarianism and workers' control in the economy. Lenin responded by putting the 'left-wing' communists in inverted commas and by telling them that they were merely more impatient than he, and more doctrinaire. By 1920 the government had to face the emergence of an authentic Workers' Opposition which demanded greater political and economic democracy. A year later there occurred a mutiny among the sailors at Kronstadt who demanded free elections to the soviets, a third revolution reminiscent in fact of the one proclaimed by the Cordeliers Club on the eve of its suppression. Trotsky, the great apostle of 'permanent revolution,' crushed the rising which he attributed to the 'counter-revolution,' an action which he continued to defend in later life. As always, there were only two alternatives: concession or repression. The Bolsheviks chose repression; with what consequences we shall see in the following chapter.

11 The revolutionary Left in power

The Soviet Union

What we have to ask about the revolutionary Left is whether its short-term dictatorial tactics have developed into a habit sufficiently endemic to obscure permanently the original quest for popular sovereignty. If so, if this were to prove the case with regard, for example, to the USSR, then it would no longer be possible to regard the Soviet régime as left-wing.

Confining our field of survey to Europe alone, the communist states provide the main evidence; both the Jacobin and Spanish anarcho-syndicalist revolutions were guillotined early on and so provide no evidence beyond the revolutionary context.

During the revolutionary phase the Bolsheviks were responsible for two developments which were destined to dominate the subsequent history of Soviet Russia: the Party's acquisition of a monopoly of power, and the concentration of that power at the top of the Party. The theoretical separation between the Party and the State was obviated in practice by the duplication of functions. A small Politburo made decisions which were automatically executed by the state administration. The Party (which expanded from 115,000 members in January 1918 to nearly 7,000,000 in 1952) not only achieved complete control and influence in all aspects of life and work, it also became for the élite an instrument with which to manipulate the base. By 1937, eighty-one per cent of the elected representatives in the Supreme Soviet were Party members and over ninety per cent of the judges were Party or Komsomol members. These figures speak for themselves.

If the Party rules, the working class rules; that is the theory. But in practice the growth of a self-sufficient bureaucracy proves to be the basic contradiction in the construction of socialism. In 1917 Lenin had envisaged that in the transitional phase from capitalism to socialism all officials would be elected on a genuinely popular basis. Under civil war conditions this ideal was, of course, not practicable. But in 1921 (when Lenin confessed openly that he was disturbed by the rearing of bureaucratism's ugly head) the Party had to choose whether or not to make a permanent virtue out of a

Stalin with the writer Maxim Gorky, the pioneer of 'socialist realism' in literature, at the Lenin mausoleum. The early revolutionary leaders adopted the plain tunic and cap as a mark of allegiance to the proletariat and of personal humility.

The Shining Light, a painting by the Russian artist M. Mariasch. The subject of this adulatory, quasi-religious portrait is, in fact, the short, square and calculating Georgian who called himself J. V. Stalin. The painting illustrates the disastrous consequences of the intrusion of the cult of personality in the artistic domain.

temporary necessity. Trotsky, Radek and Bukharin shouted down Anna Kollontai and the Workers' Opposition, and in 1923 Zinoviev admitted (or boasted) that the dictatorship of the proletariat could now be regarded as synonymous with the dictatorship of the Central Committee of the Party.

The growth of bureaucracy was represented in the early 1920's by the strengthening of the Secretariat of the Central Committee and by the progressive concentration of a wide variety of vital functions in the person of the First Secretary – J. V. Stalin. By 1925 Stalin had 767 full-time employees working under him in the Secretariat. Co-option from above increasingly replaced elections from below and elections were transformed into formal devices of assent, usually unanimous. Stalin stood at the apex of a pyramid of regional and local Party secretaries whose loyalty to him personally was commensurate with their dependence on his good will. Lenin, who fully appreciated the danger, but who was crippled by illness, made plain his aversion to Stalin in his will, a document which would have doomed Stalin in 1924 had Trotsky appreciated the full extent of the danger and acted decisively. He failed to do so; the will was suppressed; thereafter Stalin was impregnable.

Originally the Cheka was formed to crush the counter-revolution in the extraordinary circumstances of the Civil War. But it did not wither away, it assumed a more sinister institutional function in the shape of the GPU and the NKVD, a political police at the service of an oligarchy, a Red Gestapo to whose 'cruel and inhuman tortures' Khrushchev himself referred in 1956. In the 'twenties Stalin relied on his control of the Party apparatus to eliminate his opponents, first Trotsky, Zinoviev and the Left Opposition, then, subsequently, the Right, those who had supported him against Trotsky – Bukharin, Rykov and Tomsky. Before 1934 the vanquished Bolsheviks were not in general harmed physically (although Trotsky was forced into exile), but in that year the political police and the terror began to be employed against the Party itself.

Paradoxically, many found it difficult to associate Stalin's apparently modest personality with dictatorial designs, and it was

the more flamboyant and articulate Trotsky who was suspected of Bonapartism. Sidney and Beatrice Webb returned from a visit to Russia with the verdict: 'we do not think that the Party is governed by the will of a single person, or that Stalin is the sort of person to claim or desire such a position.' Naturally not; the eye sees only what it is trained to see. Unlike Napoleon, Louis Bonaparte, Mussolini and Hitler, Stalin was the first of the modern dictators to have been the creation rather than the creator of a political system, and the first also to have been avowedly a man of the Left. Stalin was, of course, personally responsible for much that took place (it may never be possible to determine exactly *how* responsible), but his final role was equally the logical outcome of the initial narrowing of the pyramid of power and of the difficulties of building socialism in so backward an economy as Russia's. The extent of his power need not be doubted. Eighteen years elapsed between the Eighteenth and Nineteenth Party Congresses (1939–52). Throughout the war the Plenum of the Central Committee was summoned together not once, and in later years, if we are to believe Khrushchev, the Politburo itself rarely met in full, Stalin having created quintets and sextets on the principle of 'divide and rule.'

Stalin, we have said, was the first dictator of the Left. But what of Robespierre? His attitude, it is true, had in some senses fore-shadowed Stalin's, although he never attained anything resembling

Stalin's personal power, nor did he desire it. In May 1793 he warned that, 'having received from the people the mandate to defend its rights, I regard as oppressor him who interrupts me . . .'. Stalin likewise condemned his rivals as 'enemies of the working class.' Robespierre held that the leader must educate the people and eliminate evil before the true popular will could emerge. Stalin gave this attitude a Marxist slant and simultaneously distorted Marxism by insisting that the consciousness of only a few moved ahead of and therefore moulded events, whereas the consciousness of the masses merely mechanically reflected the events themselves. Stalin would have agreed with Robespierre's assertion that, 'a patriot upholds the Republic *en masse*, he who opposes it on details is a traitor.' Maurice Merleau-Ponty commented in 1947 that 'every opponent is a traitor, but every traitor is only an opponent.'

Robespierre had fostered the Cult of the Supreme Being in order to stimulate cohesion among conflicting social forces and give the revolution a basis of metaphysical legitimacy. Stalin, with a similar purpose in mind, almost equated himself with the Supreme Being. In November 1936 *Pravda* described him as 'the genius of the new world, the wisest man of the epoch . . .' and mentioned his name eighty-eight times in a single issue. The cult had its foreign adherents as well. The Spanish communist Dolores Ibarruri commented that, 'to be a disciple of Stalin and a vehicle of Stalin's policy is an honour for every proletarian . . .'

It is obvious that the cult of Stalin revealed a profound lack of faith in the creativity and reliability of the proletariat and that for this reason it turned Marxism on its head. It also accompanied the removal of a good many heads. In the great purges of the late 'thirties the rational and the irrational merge beyond comprehension. Desiring to rid himself of the Old Bolsheviks, the veterans who were not his creatures, Stalin staged a series of show-trials in which the evidence was rigged and the verdicts prepared in advance. Zinoviev and Kamenev were accused of organising a 'terrorist centre' under Trotsky's guidance; Radek and others were charged with having plotted to dismember the USSR in the interests of

The face of oppression. Lavrenti Beria, a henchman of Stalin's who became chief of the political police in Russia in 1939 following the liquidation of his two predecessors, themselves adept liquidators. Beria's own execution did not follow until 1953, when death had finally removed his patron from the scene.

Germany and Japan; Bukharin elaborately confessed to an almost Satanic animosity against the revolution. Controversies raged in the West as to how the confessions were obtained. Of all the explanations, that contained in Arthur Koestler's *Darkness at Noon* – Koestler depicts a combination of physical, psychological and political pressures – probably came closest to the truth. In 1956 Khrushchev referred to the 'application of physical methods of pressurising him (the accused) . . . deprivation of his judgment, taking away of his human dignity . . . In this manner "confessions" were acquired.' Later, in 1949, the same macabre charade was played out on a minor scale in Hungary and Bulgaria. Rehabilitations followed.

But if the trials themselves had, in a sense, 'rational' motives, the purges which accompanied them and of which they were only a single manifestation carried politics far beyond the limits of logical explanation. Of a total of 139 members and candidate members of the Central Committee in 1934, ninety-eight had been executed by 1938. In June 1937 the arrest was announced of leading military figures headed by the Civil War veteran Marshal Tukachevsky. The purge struck down three of the five Red Army marshals; thirteen of the fifteen army commanders; fifty-seven of the eighty-five corps commanders; all eleven vice-commissars for war; seventy-five of the eighty members of the Supreme Military Council. But the blood-letting did not stop short here; no one, however humble a citizen, was immune. Louis Fischer, a resident in Moscow, recalled the nightmare summer of 1937: 'suicides multiplied. Youth took refuge in cynicism. Everybody played for safety first . . . to divert attention from yourself you accused the other fellow.'

In republican Spain the same mechanism of fratricidal repression came into operation, directed particularly at the anarchists and the POUM. The latter, a quasi-Trotskyist body, was in fact small and in no way a threat to republican solidarity, but for the communists purges had become a habit. In the first week of May 1937 the communists precipitated a state of war in Barcelona, the stronghold of the anarchists and the POUM alike, following up their victory with a systematic purge. The POUM leader Andrés Nin was among the thousands arrested; he was later murdered by Soviet agents. 'No measures,' declared Dolores Ibarruri, 'will ever prove excessive that are taken to purge the proletarian camp of the poisonous growth of Trotskyism . . .' It was, however, characteristic of Stalinism that the liquidators should in turn be liquidated – this was the fate of many of the Soviet personnel working in Spain.

As the terror moved towards its climax, Stalin issued in 1936 a new Constitution which was, on the face of things, a prescription for an advanced popular sovereignty. The USSR was a federation; each Union Republic enjoyed the 'right freely to secede' (untrue). The Council of Ministers required ratification by the elected Supreme Soviet to which it was responsible (a mockery; who, in any case, was to ratify Stalin who held at that time no position in the government?). The people had a right to work, to maintenance in old age and sickness, to education and sex equality (all of which had some foundation in reality). They were also entitled to freedom of conscience, of speech, of the press, of assembly and of demonstration (a joke, obviously). The individual and his home were inviolable (!). The Party was only one of several organisations having the right to nominate candidates for elections (but since the Party dominated all the others, this pluralism was illusory).

Here, with regard to our definition of the Left, the problem reaches its climax. The Constitution was both a system of government and a bill of rights. The system of government did not in reality safeguard the rights. On the contrary, it systematically violated them. The juxtaposition of the real (in many ways hardly less a denial of popular sovereignty than was Nazi Germany) and of the reiterated ideal (which fascism at its most hypocritical could never have brought itself to proclaim) created a paradox founded on three dimensions: after eighteen years of Bolshevik rule the Russian people lacked sovereignty; but their rulers continued to proclaim ardently the ideal of the extreme Left; and in the future, after 1953, the element of popular sovereignty was to come visibly into the ascendant.

Such paradoxes and fine distinctions may not count for much for the victims, for the prisoners in the forced labour camps, for the Karachai and the population of the autonomous Kalmyk Republic who were deported in 1943, for the Jews whose Yiddish publications and theatre were closed in 1949. A belief in popular sovereignty and certain types of racial prejudice are in theory compatible, but to practise racial discrimination and persecution as the anti-Semitic Stalin did is another matter. In 1952 most of the leaders of Jewish culture in Russia were shot. A trial at Prague in November of that year resulted in the prearranged condemnation of eleven prominent figures, eight of whom were Jews, for supposedly assisting a world-wide Zionist–Jewish conspiracy against socialism. Persecutions in East Germany and Hungary followed.

The Popular Democracies

The fact that the first eight years of the Sovietisation of eastern Europe coincided with Stalin's continuing dominance must largely account for the fidelity with which the Russian pattern of development was echoed in the Popular Democracies. The primary task was to eliminate *de facto* all rival parties.

In Poland, communists quickly seized key positions in the police and army, assisted by the Red Army. In the elections of October 1946, the lists of candidates presented by the Polish People's Party were disqualified in ten out of fifty-two districts, and in the following year the Party's leader, Mikolajczyk, by no means a reactionary, was forced to leave the country. In Hungary, relentless pressure was applied to the Small Farmers' Party and the National Peasant Party. The communists (who on a joint electoral list with the socialists polled only seventeen per cent of the votes in 1947) were able, again as a result of the Russian occupation, to control the security police (AVO) from the outset. In April 1948 the Party's drive for power culminated in the dissolution of parliament and in the holding of 'elections' on the basis of a single, communist-dominated government list. In Bulgaria, where the elections of November 1945 were held in an atmosphere of terror and where the results were most probably falsified, the 'Fatherland Front' rode roughshod over all opposition. Petkov, a leader of the Agrarian Union, was condemned to death by three communist judges, and in November 1948 the socialist leader Lulcher was imprisoned for refusing to toe the line. The Czechoslovak Communist Party, which began by respecting democratic forms and which was sufficiently popular to secure thirty-eight per cent of the votes in the free elections of May 1946, eventually acted true to type and exploited its influence in the police force and in the factories to carry through a *coup* early in 1948. Elections without opposition candidates inevitably ensued.

It has to be remembered that, with the single exception of Czechoslovakia, there was no tradition of democracy in eastern

Europe. The pre-war régimes had been mainly of the crypto-fascist type and based on semi-feudal agrarian economies. Hungarian society was in 1945 impregnated with fascism at all levels, and the Small Farmers' Party was no exception. In Cardinal Mindszenty not only communism but the whole principle of social justice faced an intransigent enemy who opposed the much-needed land reform on the grounds that it would undermine the revenue from which the Church maintained its control over sixty per cent of all Hungarian schools. It had, indeed, been a deliberate policy of pre-war governments in the area to limit the number of children receiving secondary education. The Popular Democracies rapidly opened up education to the working and peasant classes. In Poland, for example, only 4,600 students had scholarships in 1937; by 1951 the figure had grown to 64,540. In this context it is perhaps worth pointing out that while criticism of the Popular Democracies from a democratic standpoint is healthy, many of the most vehement critics have been those who found in the pre-war, right-wing dictatorships cause neither for complaint nor even for comment.

The Stalinist appetite for power is absolute; the defeat of the counter-revolution alone does not assuage it; all rival left-wing groups must be either absorbed or extinguished. Of the east European social democratic leaders, Kelemen was arrested in Czechoslovakia, Puzak in Poland, Petrescu in Rumania, Pastukhov in Bulgaria. The socialists were systematically 'persuaded' to fuse with the communists and so commit collective suicide. This was the fate of the Rumanian socialists in January 1948, of the Czechs in April, of the Hungarians in June, of the Poles in December and of the Bulgarians in the same month. Simultaneously, the more 'liberal' elements in the Communist Parties were replaced in key positions by the hard Stalinists. Gomulka, who was known to stand for greater Polish independence, was officially disgraced and gave way to Beirut and Berman, while in Hungary the Stalinists Rákosi and Gerö constructed a political edifice which rested on the backs of 150,000 political prisoners, 2,000 of whom are believed to have been executed.

The Hungarian revolution, October–November 1956. Demonstrators burn a portrait of the hated Party boss Rákosi in the streets of Budapest. Like his mentor Stalin, Rákosi carried political oppression to such lengths as to obliterate any vestige of popular sovereignty.

In eastern Europe the post-Stalin thaw proved less easy to graduate and control than in Russia itself. In Poland disaster was averted. A strike among the workers of Poznan in June 1956 and the anti-Russian demonstrations which ensued led to wage concessions and to the return of the more liberal Gomulka as General Secretary of the Party. Six Stalinists were removed from the Politburo. It was the Polish demonstrations, following as they did Khrushchev's denunciation of Stalin in February, which sparked off the Hungarian revolution in October. The popular communist Imre Nagy became Premier. The Russians, who had themselves been responsible for the removal of Rákosi, decided, after some hesitation, to withdraw the Red Army units from Budapest and to let events run their course. But a Stalinist faction headed by Gerö and the security police resisted, generating counter-violence and a revolution which became 'permanent' in an unusual dialectical form; a simultaneous drive towards greater popular sovereignty and national independence on the one hand and towards frankly anti-socialist elements on the other. On 30 October Nagy announced the abolition of the one-party system, the inclusion in his government of non-communists like Béla Kovács, Zoltán Tildy and Anna Kéthly, and – the last straw for the Russians – the withdrawal of Hungary from the Warsaw Pact into neutrality. At the same time voices calling for Western intervention began to be heard from clandestine radio stations (of this there is no doubt). For all this the Russians had only themselves to blame; in eleven years they and their minions had failed to make of communism a system acceptable to the vast majority of the Hungarian people. Nagy's withdrawal from the Warsaw Pact was, however, a foolish and precipitate gesture. Hungary, like Rumania, had joined Nazi Germany in a war of unprovoked aggression against the USSR in 1941, and in the conditions of the Cold War the Russians were unlikely to allow her to float diplomatically adrift. The Red Army now intervened in the most brutal manner and Budapest was bombarded into submission. Dissidence was systematically repressed and Nagy, who had been arrested, was later executed.

The case of Yugoslavia requires a separate analysis. In Yugoslavia alone did communism take power as the result of a genuinely indigenous and popularly supported revolution. Separated from and threatened by the Soviet bloc from 1948 until 1955, the Yugoslav régime self-consciously applied itself to avoid the dictatorial features which blemished Stalinism. A relatively democratic system of government was evolved to balance the leading role of the Party. The basic unit of government is the Commune, the governing body of which consists of two chambers of equal status, the Communal Council (elected by universal suffrage) and the Council of Producers (representing the Workers' Councils of the enterprises within the Commune). At the national level, the same system is duplicated: the Federal Council (elected by universal suffrage) and the Federal Council of Producers together elect the Federal Executive Council whose President is also President of the Republic. If the Party's role within and above this complex organism is, as was admitted at the Ljubljana Congress in 1958, a dictatorial one, emphasis is nevertheless laid on the progressive diminution of its role and on the 'withering away' of the state. On the probability of such a development judgment can only be conjectural. Two negative factors demand attention: firstly, Tito's personal position in the State has remained hardly less prominent

Belgrade, 1948, on the eve of Yugoslavia's rupture with the USSR.
The outsize portraits of Lenin, Tito and Stalin were soon to be reduced
to one of Tito alone. Stalin failed in his attempt to bully Yugoslavia
in the spirit of great-power chauvinism. Yet in Yugoslavia, for all
its emphasis on internal democratisation, the cult of Tito's
personality has not waned.

than Stalin's (although there the parallel ends); secondly, the régime's tolerance of criticism has been put in doubt by the imprisonment of the dissenting writer Milovan Djilas.

Cultural policy

The fate of Djilas raises the general question of communist policy towards literature, scholarship and the arts. In precise terms, censorship as such is not incompatible with popular sovereignty. The sovereign people might, for example, decide to protect their young from pornography, or they might ban racist or other types of literature which they find repugnant. The question, in the present context of discussion, is: *who* applies the censorship?

In May 1921, the Soviet Commissar for Public Instruction, A. Lunacharsky, foreshadowed the shape of things to come when he wrote: 'we in no way shrink from the necessity of applying censorship even to *belles-lettres*, since under this banner . . . poison may be implanted in the still naïve and dark souls of the great mass of the people.' But the threat was not fully implemented until the 'thirties. Trotsky observed that the Party could not and would not dominate art 'by means of decrees and orders,' and in May 1924 the Party formally reserved its neutrality towards the rival literary trends. Stalin was not the man to maintain such scruples. In 1932 he described writers as 'engineers of human souls,' and two years later the fully elaborated doctrine of socialist realism was defined as 'the basic method of Soviet *belles-lettres* and literary criticism,' which demanded of the writer a 'truthful, historically concrete representation of reality in its revolutionary development.' In practice this meant a literature impregnated with '*partiinost*' – the spirit of the Party, a literature lavish in its praise of Stalin. A. A. Zhdanov became the virtual dictator of the Soviet cultural scene. Art for art's sake, western 'formalism' and any tendency towards abstractionism were ceaselessly denounced after the war. Literature did not suffer alone. Intoxicated by his power, the philistine Zhdanov carried his terror campaigns into the realms of philosophy, philology and even music. In 1948 he inspired a Central Committee decree which accused a number of eminent compòsers, including Prokofiev, Shostakovich and Khachaturian, of anti-democratic formalism and insisted that they model their work on the Russian classics.

It was at this time that official bullying reached the point of absurdity when the Party dogmatically intervened in a strictly technical controversy among geneticists on the question of the inheritance of acquired characteristics. When the botanist T. D. Lysenko revealed at a session of the Academy of Agricultural Sciences that his theories (which by analogy appeared to be politically useful) had official endorsement, certain of his opponents hypnotically and spontaneously recanted, declaring themselves unworthy of the name of Soviet scientist, etc. Twelve professors and academicians were dismissed for their obduracy and remained in obscurity until it was admitted a few years later that Lysenko's theories were not after all verifiable. This little drama recalls, perhaps, Bertolt Brecht's play *Galileo*. Brecht depicts the ruling orthodoxy (the Church) proscribing a scientific theory as dangerous; Stalin stood the precedent on its head, sanctifying a scientific theory because it seemed useful. It was doubtless with his tongue in his cheek that Brecht journeyed to Moscow to receive a Stalin Prize.

Russia is a country rich in inventive genius. Yet under Bolshevik rule Mayakovsky committed suicide, Babel was one of hundreds of writers who died in camps, Meyerhold's theatre was closed down and its creator liquidated, Pasternak ended his days in disgrace and Eisenstein saw his film *Ivan the Terrible* mutilated. The repressive atmosphere could only lead to what Sholokov called in 1954 'the dreary torrent of colourless, mediocre literature . . . flooding our book market.' It is not surprising that Soviet cultural achievements have been concentrated in non-ideological spheres, in the performing and instrumental arts, in the ballet, in science and mathematics, in the teaching of languages. These qualitative advances reflect quantitative progress in the provision of education. Communism is strong on welfare and weak on freedom.

Economic policy

Marx failed to tackle the problems of distribution and exchange in a socialist society and he failed also to consider at what level and by what mechanism planning would take place. The Bolsheviks, in search of a coherent economic policy, were compelled to mix a large dose of pragmatism with a few grains of Marxist guidance, a dose doubly hard to administer since the Russian economy in 1917, even had it not been devastated by war, would not have attained the stage of development at which Marx had envisaged a socialist transformation. Confronted by the obvious antithesis between centralised planning and localised workers' control, the Bolsheviks opted, characteristically, for planning.

Until the summer of 1918 factories tended to be supervised by workers' councils who acted independently and with little regard for the needs of a co-ordinated economy. Although Lenin succeeded in curbing this syndicalist spirit with an empirical regard for productive efficiency, over-riding the protests of the Left Communists in the process, the onset of the Civil War led to the introduction of a new system, 'War Communism,' the foundations of which were far from empirical. The workers were paid in kind, wages were dispensed with as far as possible and the free market likewise, labour was militarised in conformity with the *Communist Manifesto*'s prediction of the 'establishment of industrial armies, especially for agriculture.' This system, theoretically the work of Larin and Kritsmann, was less a pragmatic response to war conditions than was subsequently claimed. To a large extent it was a utopian attempt to realise full communism immediately, and to forestall the degeneration of the revolution.

Its practical defects outweighed its idealistic virtues. A strategical retreat was ordered in 1921 in the shape of the New Economic Policy under which private enterprise was restored in the countryside, certain nationalised industries were leased to the private sector and the currency was stabilised. The worker may not have become sovereign but at least he enjoyed a few years' respite from the serfdom which preceded and followed the NEP. But socialism would not develop of its own accord. In 1928 Stalin took the plunge which Trotsky had long since urged, the leap to the left, and launched the first Five Year Plan to rescue the revolution from stagnation, to increase industrial productivity and to create, so it was hoped, the large agricultural surpluses needed for feeding the growing towns. The Five Year Plans differed from War Communism in four main respects: money was in circulation, the consumer was free to buy, the labour market was based on incentives and differentials, and planning took the place of *ad hoc* measures.

Labour – that is to say millions of working men and women – was simultaneously fed the carrot and shown the whip. The carrot was not in fact widely digestible, taking as it did the form of high bonuses and rewards for the 'Stakhanovites,' the most productive workers. The 'whip' assumed a variety of forms. In the period 1926–39, 24,000,000 people migrated from the land to the urban centres, a migration which was by no means uniformly voluntary. The trade unions, deprived of all autonomy, acted as recruiting agents. In an attempt to check the flow of labour moving on in search of better-paid jobs, internal passports were introduced in 1932. 'Deserters' were deprived of their ration cards and of their claim to living quarters. Thus the Bolsheviks introduced what the French revolution of 1848 had been so proud to abolish almost a century earlier – workers' passports. The Russian worker's freedom to leave his factory now depended on the 'triangle,' the director of the enterprise, the president of the union committee and the secretary of the Party cell. In theory a member of the ruling class, the worker could no longer command even his own two feet.

The 'whip' had many strands. The peasantry as a whole obstinately resisted and obstructed collectivisation. There is no doubt that under the NEP the kulaks had been holding back grain surpluses in order to hold the towns to ransom. In embarking upon collectivisation the Bolsheviks hoped to avoid a direct struggle between town and country and to harness the poorer peasants and landless labourers to the proletarian camp in accordance with Lenin's original analysis. But this was not to be. Rather than have them expropriated, the kulaks slaughtered their cattle. In the period 1928–34, the number of horses, cattle and pigs declined by about half, and the number of sheep by two-thirds. It was a disaster. The Bolsheviks responded with desperation and resorted to police terror on an unprecedented scale. In areas like Smolensk any peasant, whatever his status or conduct, was liable to arrest and thereafter either to deportation or death, or both.

Thus collectivisation and the political purges produced in combination a vast pool of manpower which was transported to camps, administered by a subdivision of the NKVD and converted into forced labour. Prisoners were set to work felling timber, building roads and canals, working in the mines. There is evidence to show that in the late 1930's there existed between 7,000,000 and 14,000,000 Russians working in such camps, at least 125 of which can be located and named, along with their main economic activities. One authority estimates that about sixteen per cent of all Russian adult males were confined in camps in the immediate post-war period. If, in these circumstances, the Soviet people were in any sense sovereign, they were truly remarkable for their masochism.

There is no objective criterion by which these terrible hardships, the sacrifice of consumer goods of the most basic kind to heavy industry, and the deliberately lowered standard of living (real wages in terms of the food price index had by 1936–7 fallen to half their 1928 level) can be measured against the enormous increase of productivity, the full employment at a time of world economic crisis, the creation of a war machine which was able to repel the German invader. The two sets of values which these lists imply are not comparable; the sacrifice of one generation cannot be measured against the salvation of the next, even if it could be proven beyond doubt that this salvation demanded such inhumane methods.

The Popular Democracies were, with the notable exception of Czechoslovakia, economically retarded by western standards and therefore susceptible to the same combination of shock-tactics and the artificial acceleration of development which had taken place in the USSR. The long-term industrial plans put into operation in these countries after 1948 envisaged the investment of between twenty and twenty-five per cent of the national income on expansion. As in Russia, female labour was mobilised on a large scale, the more productive workers received innumerable welfare benefits, and consumer goods were sacrificed to the needs of heavy industry. In this respect the Cold War provided an urgent military incentive as the Nazi threat to Russia had done in the 'thirties. In Hungary the strain thrown on the working class contributed to the complex of political and economic tensions which coalesced in the revolution of 1956.

Yugoslav communism, compelled and enabled by Soviet hostility to make its own revisionist *critique* of the Stalinist social structure, applied fresh thinking to the problem raised by the tendency of state ownership of the means of production to lead to an indefinite preservation of the state-hired labour relationship. The Yugoslavs discovered that the guided reintroduction of a free market can check the Stalinisation of the economy, that competition between enterprises is compatible with socialism, and that nationalisation need not in itself imply the creation of monopolies.

An equally distinctive feature of communist economic policy in Yugoslavia has been its emphasis on workers' control – on genuine popular sovereignty in the economic sphere. The management of a Yugoslav enterprise is vested by law in its Workers' Council. The Councils, which were established in 1950, are elected by secret ballot every two years from and by members of the collective. According to official figures, 117,965 of the 154,454 members of the Workers' Councils in 1960 were manual workers. Of these, skilled workers comprised just over half. The Council in turn elects a Managing Board, a majority of whose members are also workers. The Council can take the initiative in calling for the dismissal of the director of an enterprise, although the unions may then intervene and sustain the case of either party. There is, unfortunately, evidence which suggests a marked discrepancy between Yugoslav theory and practice. Not until 1964 was the right to strike

legalised, and the actual power of the Councils, as compared with the power wielded by the Party and government, has been less extensive than official propaganda would claim.

The pattern of agricultural development in the Popular Democracies also echoed the Soviet model, although free from the excessive human sacrifices. In the first instance the land was redistributed; collectivisation did not begin until 1949–50. The operation was not on the whole a success. The Polish peasants, like the Russians before them, resisted by sabotage, hoarding and passive non-obedience. The vast majority of Polish collectives disappeared with the rebellion of 1956. Centuries of land-hunger have shaped the peasant mentality. The poor or landless peasant supports a régime which benefits him at the expense of his wealthier neighbour or landlord. But – and here is the paradox – even those without land tend to resist the complete abolition of private property in land because a dream, a hope, the aspiration which is the basis of life and labour, is thereby permanently destroyed.

Left: Russia, 1921, in the aftermath of the civil war. Having won this struggle, the Bolsheviks set about establishing a monopolistic grip on every aspect of social, political and, ultimately, cultural life. Here a propaganda train is seen touring the provinces. *Right*: A Soviet woman bricklayer. The mobilisation of female labour on a large scale has been a key element in the USSR's construction and industrialisation programmes. Children below school age are well taken care of by the local authorities during the day so as to enable their mothers to work.

Anarchism in Spain

But is this invariably the case? One particular European episode associated with the advent to power of the revolutionary Left throws doubt on the universality of this aspect of the peasant mentality. The period of the Spanish Civil War was marked by the creation of about 1,500 collectives in Catalonia, Aragon, Levante and Andalusia, their strengths varying from 5,000 to 100 members. The primary ideological influence here was, of course, anarchist, although the socialist UGT co-operated in a number of instances.

To what extent these collectives were voluntary and spontaneous creations is a question to which no single answer can be found. In the South, where landless labourers outnumbered peasant proprietors, collectivisation almost automatically accompanied the expropriation of the large estates. Quite often smallholders joined voluntarily, bringing their land, livestock and tools to the collective; on other occasions, as at Seriñena, they confined their co-operation to the pooling of machinery. But elsewhere there is abundant evidence of coercion by anarchist militia units like the Durutti column which adopted a 'collectivise or die' approach.

Of the influence of the great anarchist theorists, it is again difficult to generalise. The internal economy of the collectives tended to combine Bakunin's and Kropotkin's principles of remuneration; wage rates were based partly on needs and partly on work performed. Bread, potatoes, olive oil and sometimes wine were in many cases distributed free. The total abolition of wages was sometimes followed by their gradual reappearance. Distinctly anarchistic in their resolute hostility to the state and in their emphasis on local self-sufficiency, the collectives were more ambiguously libertarian with regard to their internal structure. In one collective the General Assembly might meet every week; in another the elected Council of Administration tended to monopolise authority.

The Spanish anarchists embarked on their revolutionary drive with equal ardour in the industrial sphere – the single occasion, brief though it was, when anarcho-syndicalism was granted the opportunity to put its theories into practice. On 24 October 1936, the Generalitat of Catalonia collectivised all enterprises of more than 100 workers. In Barcelona, banks, hotels and some factories had already been expropriated and placed under the control of workers' committees. The railways and public services were run by committees of the CNT and UGT. Any scientific evaluation of the overall efficiency of the experiment is frustrated by circumstantial factors, particularly the hostility of the communists and the brevity of the experiment itself. The smaller factories appear to have been run successfully and harmoniously, but the larger war industries either lagged behind their targets or became dependent on technical advisers who were often communists and therefore out of sympathy with the experiment. Above all, the Madrid government learned in time to throttle the Catalonian factories by withholding supplies of raw materials. For this reason the industrial collectives died a quicker death than their agrarian counterparts.

12 The reformist Left in power

The revolutionary Left in power, we have suggested, is strong on welfare and weak on freedom. The evidence indicates that the reformist Left in power is also strong on welfare but weak on popular sovereignty. In its quest for power, the one sacrifices liberty; by its respect for liberty, the other sacrifices power. This point is easily illustrated. In the ninety-odd years since its foundation, the German Socialist Party has at no time gained an absolute parliamentary majority or been able to govern from a commanding position. The French Socialist Party, which was unified sixty years ago, attained a leading position in coalition governments for approximately two years in all; it has never ruled. The Italian Socialist Party is more than seventy years old, yet Italy has never had a socialist government. The record of the Spanish Socialist Party is only marginally more impressive. Another creation of the nineteenth century, the British Labour Party, had up to 1964 ruled for six years and governed without a parliamentary majority for a further three. Only in Sweden has reformist socialism gained anything resembling a permanent grip on the reins of power.

Paradoxically, this prolonged and universal impotence reflects a hidden achievement. Only by constant retreats, constant concessions and opportunist compromises have the Right and Centre been able to retain their political dominance in western Europe. In the context of parliamentary democracy (although not under right-wing dictatorships) the reformist Left has emerged as a highly effective permanent opposition.

The primary achievements of the reformist and democratic Left are associated with the modern welfare state. During their brief period of power (1918–20), the Austrian socialists were able to sustain a reasonably high level of wages and unemployment relief while taking effective measures to check unemployment. In Sweden the first homogeneous socialist government took office in 1920, and in subsequent years the socialists were responsible for increasing pensions and unemployment relief, for reducing working hours, and for introducing maternity benefits and a national medical service. Per Albin Hansson's government initiated an

White tie and tails. The second
Social Democrat government in Sweden.
which lasted from December 1921
until April 1923. H. Branting,
Prime Minister and Foreign Minister,
is seated in the middle.

extensive public works programme which had a remarkable
success in alleviating unemployment in the 1930's. The Labour
government of 1924 in Britain was responsible for an act whereby
the state subsidised the building of council houses. The Attlee
governments of 1945–51 raised the school leaving age to fifteen,
took some measures to improve the appalling condition of public
education in Britain, introduced compulsory national insurance
and created an excellent National Health Service providing free
drugs and medical treatment. The Popular Front government of
1936 in France secured for the workers a considerable wage
increase, supported the principle of collective bargaining and
introduced the forty-hour week.

But on the issue of popular sovereignty in the economic sphere the general impression is one of timidity, retreat, compromise and, occasionally, betrayal. Strong as their position was after 1918, the German socialists made no serious attempt to smash the hold of the old imperial administrative class on the army, the bureaucracy and the judiciary. The large estates east of the Elbe, the heartland of the reactionary Prussian nobility, escaped unscathed. The government refused to meet the miners' appeal for the nationalisation of the coal mines, and Rudolf Wissell, the advocate of a planned and socialised economy, was duly forced out of his office as Minister of the National Economy in 1919 by his socialist colleagues. The German economy remained under private control; it was from the great industrial barons that the Nazis were later to derive the financial assistance without which they could not have seized power.

Ramsey MacDonald's government did not enjoy the support of a Labour majority in the House of Commons in 1924; indeed five out of seven voters were committed to the Conservative and Liberal Parties. MacDonald faced two alternatives; to pursue a recognisably socialist policy, to be defeated in Parliament and, very probably, to strengthen the Labour Party's position among the working class at the subsequent elections; or, alternatively, to compromise. He chose to compromise. Only two left-wing Labour men were included in his cabinet; a Tory was made First Lord of the Admiralty; and MacDonald assured the King that he was trying to curb the habit among Labour MP's of singing the *Red Flag*. Labour leaders and their wives revelled in court ceremonies. J. R. Clynes later recalled: 'as we stood waiting for His Majesty, amid the gold and crimson of the Palace, I could not help marvelling at the strange turn of Fortune's Wheel . . .'. Little was done to alleviate unemployment. Confronted by strikes among transport workers, the government, to the horror of its supporters and of the trade union movement, resorted to the Emergency Powers Act which the Labour Party itself had vehemently denounced when Lloyd George introduced it four years earlier.

The record of the second Labour government of 1929–31, when measured against the gravity of the economic situation, was even worse. By the autumn of 1930 the number of unemployed exceeded 2,000,000. Oswald Mosley's proposals – state control of foreign trade and the expansion of the government's purchasing powers – were rejected by the Chancellor of the Exchequer, Philip Snowden, who followed the advice of the orthodox Treasury officials and who was determined, in the best classical manner, to balance his budget. The government turned in desperation to the American bankers J. P. Morgan & Co, who made a loan to the Bank of England conditional on government-inspired economies. MacDonald, supported by Snowden, favoured a ten per cent cut in unemployment benefits. When he encountered opposition within the cabinet, MacDonald promptly resigned and, without warning the majority of his colleagues or the Party, put himself at the head of a coalition government of Conservatives and Liberals. The Labour Party did not recover from this blow for more than a decade.

The record of the Attlee government which took office in 1945 was much more impressive. It needed to be; the Labour Party now had an overall majority of 146 seats in the Commons. Even so, the venerable legacy of endemic caution lived on. In April 1945, the Party's election manifesto warned that 'socialism cannot come overnight . . . ,' a sentiment with which it would be difficult to quarrel; but when in 1950 the Party confined its proposals for further nationalisation to sugar, cement and the water supply, it was no longer clear whether socialism would ever come. To what extent had the government brought the economy under popular control?

The Bank of England had been nationalised, a measure which even the Conservative Party did not oppose. When the state took over the coal mines their owners were clearly pleased to be relieved of a financial liability and at the same time to be so generously compensated. The same applied to the railways. The nationalisation of the cable and wireless companies were merely the logical conclusion of a policy adopted by earlier governments. Electricity and gas were also nationalised, but they too were already under substantial public control. The nationalisation of road transport and of the iron and steel industries evoked considerably more opposition from the owners and the Right. The general effect of these legislative measures was not only to leave about eighty per cent of the economy under private control but also to strengthen the capitalist sector by relieving it of its money-losing industries. Britain emerged from six long years of Labour rule without a tax on property and without a tax on capital gains. The balance of property ownership had not seriously been disturbed; two per cent of the adult population possessed about fifty per cent of the total net capital. Above all, the nationalisation schemes undertaken in Britain between 1945 and 1951 entailed no concession at all to the principle of workers' control. The directing boards of the nationalised industries were from the outset dominated by men closely associated with private enterprise. The Labour government evidently had no patience with utopias; in October

1946, Sir Stafford Cripps observed: 'I think it would be almost impossible to have worker-controlled industry in Britain, even if it were on the whole desirable.' When a motion was proposed at the Party Conference in 1948 calling for the nationalisation of the iron and steel industries on the basis of 'a complete scheme of control by the workers engaged in the industry,' the government turned a deaf ear.

Sweden is the country of 'the middle way.' Public and private enterprise, capital and labour, town and country work together more or less harmoniously. The principle of establishing state monopolies (which balance public control and semi-independent direction) was one which the socialists inherited and extended. The state controls the major means of transportation, the telephone and telegraph, at the same time sharing ownership of the timber industry and of electric power with private enterprise. The Social Democratic Party became, particularly after the Second World War, the dominant force in Swedish politics, but it would be a mistake to conclude that Sweden is in any real sense a socialist country. No general assault on the private sector of the economy was attempted before the last war, and subsequently schemes for nationalising the banks, oil and insurance were shelved.

French socialism has never been in a position to implement its ancient ideals even had it continued to hold them dear. When in 1937 Léon Blum demanded a tax on capital and the nationalisation of certain industries the Chamber approved but the Senate – elected on an indirect franchise and strongly favouring the rural and conservative interests – forced him to resign. On his disillusioning experiences as leader of a Popular Front majority he later had this to say:

> It is true that, despite all contrary appearances, it is the bourgeoisie which has ruled France for a century-and-a-half ... even when the elected Chamber appeared to belong to a popular majority, the bourgeoisie conserved means of resistance ... it disposed of local assemblies, of bureaucrats, of the press, of finance, of business circles, and above all of the Senate ...

PART FOUR

'Workers of all countries, unite!'

13 Nationalism and internationalism

Here again the record of the European Left is one of ambivalence and ambiguity, of confusion and contradiction. That the Left is by nature and without exception internationalist and anti-patriotic is a common belief which dissolves into dust on the most cursory examination of the evidence.

The Jacobins fought a national war in the name of international liberation. Confusing conquest with deliverance, they and their Napoleonic successors became scornful and repressive when they encountered resistance. Curiously enough, the later republicans, like the proverbial Bourbons, forgot nothing and learned nothing. Rapsail was the first republican to repudiate French claims to Belgium and Savoy. He was isolated. *Le National* rejected his ideas and the republicans continued to denounce the monarchy's peace policy as a betrayal of French claims to the left bank of the Rhine. The Treaty of Vienna, the republicans and the 'treasonous' monarchy was an equation put into reverse ideologically a century later by the Treaty of Versailles, Hitler and the 'treasonous' Weimar Republic. The exiled *Société Démocratique Française* warned that a revolutionary France would at once declare war in order to liberate the rest of Europe. Lamartine, the Foreign Minister of the Provisional Government of 1848, hastened to assure the Powers that this was not to be the case.

If the internationalist spirit dictated for sections of the French Left a war of conquest, elsewhere it represented the demand for national self-determination against the supra-national principle of the feudal monarchies. It was taken for granted that the new sovereign nations would introduce representative government and refrain from attacking their neighbours. Those Poles who had gone into exile in 1831 excited widespread sympathy, particularly in France where Louis Blanc championed their cause. Like fascism later, the absolutist Holy Alliance bound its enemies together in comradeship. The Fraternal Democrats included Germans like Moll, Marx and Schapper, English Chartists like Harney and Ernest Jones, as well as Irishmen, Frenchmen, Poles and Belgians. In 1836 the Chartist WMA sent a message of solidarity to the

Where internationalist crusading fervour becomes brutal
national oppression. Goya's great painting,
showing French soldiers in Spain executing prisoners.
The strategy of foreign conquest perfected
by Napoleon had been launched under the Jacobins –
men of the Left.

Belgian workers. London and Brussels became centres of internationalist agitation, havens for exiles. Weitling argued that only
property owners had a country of their own; the Federation of the
Just proclaimed the brotherhood of all men, and the first number
of the *Communist Review*, published in London in 1847, bore the
slogan, 'Workers of all countries, unite!'

It was the belief of Marx and Engels that only large, centralised
and independent states could take the road to socialism. But here a

problem arose; absolute adherence to the principle of self-determination in eastern Europe would lead to a multiplicity of small states. The German Left resolved the problem by surrending to its prejudices. While Marx never ceased to criticise English domination in Ireland, he regarded German domination of the Czechs as quite another matter. Czech independence was out of the question; it would leave eastern Germany looking like a loaf gnawed by rats. In 1851 Engels dismissed with contempt Slav pretensions to national independence on the ground that the German faculty for absorbtion was the best vehicle for spreading western civilisation and socialism in the East.

In so far as the German Left exercised any influence in 1848, it was only to reinforce the nationalism of the Right. The slogan 'unity, freedom and power' soon reduced itself to 'unity and power.' The demand for Polish independence initially canvassed in German left-wing circles soon evaporated when it was remembered that 700,000 Germans lived in Posnania and would therefore be subject to Polish rule. The Berlin democrat Wilhelm Jordan described the Poles as being of 'lesser cultural content' and spoke up for a 'healthy national egotism without which no people can grow into a nation . . . our right is that of the stronger, the right of conquest.' The preponderance of Germans over Slavs was, he felt, a fact of history.

Marx's nationalism was a good deal milder and more offset by a genuine internationalism than was generally the case within the German Left. He did, it is true, welcome Prussia's victory over France in 1870 as likely to have the effect of bringing Marxism to the forefront in the German and European socialist movements, but his followers abstained on the issue of voting the war credits whereas the Lassallians showed no hesitation in voting in their favour. Lassalle was first and last a nationalist; his influence, combined with Marx's political suspicion of the Slavs, re-emerged with remarkable clarity in 1914 when the SPD threw its weight behind German expansion in the East. The Kaiser, so this attitude seemed to imply, was both a liberator and an exporter of that uniquely German commodity – socialism. Even this theory lost its relevance in 1918 when the SPD deputies ratified the blatantly imperialist Treaty of Brest-Litovsk, imposed by force on a Russia which, far from labouring under the Tsarist tyranny, was now under Bolshevik control.

The history of nineteenth-century internationalism is the history of ambiguity. Garibaldi, who fought for the liberty of the South American states and who was a friend of all peoples aspiring to national independence, was, in company with Mazzini, criticised in 1866 by Bakunin as the apostle of 'that detestable theory of bourgeois patriotism . . .' Garibaldi fought the French in the cause of Italian independence; in 1870 he fought the Prussians in the cause of French independence. Garibaldi visualised a community of independent states; Bakunin demanded a world without states. Bitter experience had taught him that the nationalist movements to which he had originally been committed were not by definition socially progressive.

The Paris Commune was both nationalist and internationalist in its emotive appeal; it called simultaneously for decentralisation and national independence. The Communards, who regarded themselves as Frenchmen first and last, attracted the sympathy and support of numerous foreigners, the Hungarian Frankel, the Poles Wroblewski and Dombrowski, the Italian Amilcare Cipriani. Marx upheld Prussia against France and the Commune against both. After 1900, the Second International, constantly preoccupied with the problem of containing the forces of rampant nationalism and of keeping the peace, tried in vain to discover a way of upholding each nation against all and all nations against each.

Stalin began as he was to continue for thirty years, practising a policy of Russian nationalism and neo-colonialism on the one hand, and abandoning the internationalist revolutionary ideal on the other. This latter strategy evidently came to him as a sudden revelation. In April 1924 he was still of the opinion that socialism required proletarian dictatorships in several countries; by December he had changed his mind. 'Socialism in one country' was the

Badge of the International Brigade which fought
for the Republic in Spain during the Civil War.
Recruited from volunteers of many nationalities,
but mainly communists, the Brigade
played a heroic part in the defence of Madrid.
In 1938 it was disbanded.

new slogan, the new orthodoxy. Trotsky reminded him that in 1918 it had been no less an opinion than Lenin's that, 'without the victory of the revolution in Germany, we are doomed.'

Much the sounder Marxist, Trotsky nevertheless proclaimed his thesis from a pedestal built of false predictions. At the time of the 1905 revolution he had written: 'a war between feudal-bourgeois Germany and revolutionary Russia would inevitably lead to a proletarian revolution in Germany.' By an irony of fate, it was he who signed the Treaty of Brest-Litovsk, a painful reminder of his mistake. He had also predicted that, 'the triumph of the revolution in Russia will mean the inevitable victory of the revolution in Poland.' Here again he was mistaken; Trotsky conducted an unhappy dialogue with 'inevitability.' By 1929 he had to agree that in so far as the Bolshevik state had continued to exist in isolation for twelve years, things had not turned out quite as he and Lenin had anticipated. His basic conviction remained, however, unshakeable. 'Let there be no illusions; we have received an undated moratorium. We live as before, under the conditions of a breathing space.' He insisted that the world division of labour and the dependence of Soviet industry on foreign technology made the construction of socialism in one country impossible.

Stalin transformed the Comintern into an agent of Russia's national interests, its policies reflecting the attitude towards the capitalist states. In the late 'twenties, France was hostile, Britain broke off diplomatic relations and Germany was drifting from the Russo-German alliance. Consequently the communists in the West reverted to an anti-nationalist, anti-patriotic posture, criticising colonial imperialism and denouncing the rearmament programmes of their respective countries. But when in 1934 the Soviet Union turned towards a diplomatic *rapprochement* with the democracies, the Comintern donned a new set of clothes and began to champion nations everywhere (except in the colonies!). Dimitrov warned communists in 1935 that they must on no account permit fascism to claim unchallenged ancestors in past national heroes. The USSR, he reminded them, was socialist in content but

national in form [*sic*]. The French communists, who embraced the new line with especial fervour, and who would not tolerate any talk of abandoning even a kilometre of the French Empire, began to trace their spiritual lineage back to Joan of Arc, taking in not not only Robespierre but also Napoleon and Louis XIV *en route*.

Left-wing internationalism at its most noble (Bakuninism was noble but impossible) has been reflected in the spirit which drives a man to defend the independence and democratic liberties of any nation whatsoever. Garibaldi and the foreign Communards were of this mould; so also were those who fought in the International Brigades during the Spanish Civil War. The Brigades, organised by the Comintern and recruited from foreign volunteers, were sixty per cent communist and eighty per cent working class in composi-

Some of the 3,000 members of the International Brigade consisting of Poles, Czechs and Germans seen entering the border town of Le Perthus.
These men represented the internationalist spirit of the Left in its most noble form.

tion. Italian and German anti-fascists fought in the Garibaldi and Thaelmann Brigades and a galaxy of communist leaders descended on Spain; Marty from France, Togliatti from Italy, Tito from Yugoslavia and Gottwald from Czechoslovakia. At least twenty-nine nationalities were represented in the Brigades. The flower of the left-wing intelligentsia was drawn into the fray. The novelist André Malraux organised the Air Squadron at Aleantarilla, George Orwell fought at the front as a POUM militiaman, and the British Left sent the most ardent and talented of its young poets and literary critics, many of whom never returned. Louis Fischer, writing after his break with communism, continued to insist from first-hand experience that the majority of Russians in Spain 'could not have fought for their native land with more self-sacrifice and heroism. They identified themselves with Spain. It was their adopted country.'

The motives of the Soviet government for intervening on behalf of the Republic were doubtless self-interested, but the fact remains that Soviet self-interest at that time coincided absolutely with the defence of European democracy against fascism. Between October 1936 and April of the following year, thirty or forty Russian ships left for Spain each month laden with food, grain, oil, fertilizer, cotton, machinery, vehicles and arms. The Russians intervened whereas the French socialist Premier Léon Blum, the head of a newly elected Popular Front majority, declared 'my soul is torn' and flew promptly to London where he was lectured on the virtues of caution by the Conservative government. In France, the Radicals were on the whole against intervening in Spain, but the communists and the majority of socialists were in favour. Spain did not require French troops, only French planes and arms. But Blum closed the frontier and stood passively by while Franco, amply assisted by Germany and Italy, gradually crushed the Republic. In Britain, the National Council of Labour and the Trades Union Congress contented themselves with echoing the absurd argument that intervention, even the transportation of arms, would imply the risk of a European war. The Spanish Civil War marks both the zenith and the nadir of left-wing internationalism.

In subsequent years Stalin continued to combine profitably 'socialism in one country' with a policy of nationalist aggrandise-ment. Having signed a Pact of Non-aggression with Germany in August 1939, Russia took over her share of partitioned Poland, declared war on Finland from whom she seized the Karelian Isthmus, and incorporated Estonia, Latvia and Lithuania into the USSR. After the war Ruthenia was taken from Czechoslovakia, Bukovina and Bessarabia from Rumania. Poland as a whole was shifted westwards to Russia's advantage and Germany's cost. In the Far East the appetite had to be satisfied with such morsels as Dairen, Port Arthur and the Kiril Islands. A neo-colonialist policy in eastern Europe completed the picture.

Stalin afforded no clearer example of his determination to dominate the smaller states of eastern Europe than in his deliber-ately manufactured dispute with Yugoslavia. According to Khrushchev's account, Stalin confided: 'I will shake my little finger – and there will be no more Tito. He will fall.' Having failed in their attempt to subvert the independence of the Yugoslav army and Party and to build up an effective pro-Soviet opposition group to challenge Tito, the Russians decided in 1948 publicly to grind the Yugoslavs into submission. Although the Soviet Party was at that time the negation of democracy, and although Yugoslavia had travelled more rapidly on the road to socialism than the Russian-dominated Popular Democracies, the Russian note ex-pressed dismay at the absence of democracy within the Yugoslav Party and at the evidence of capitalistic elements in the Yugoslav economy. In subsequent years, before Khrushchev arrived in Bel-grade to make peace and to admit that the conflict had been artificially blown up, Tito was blackened by the whole communist movement as a genuine fascist in the pay of Wall Street.

Stalin, then, transformed 'socialism in one country' into 'social-ism in one power bloc' while maintaining his reluctance to en-courage genuinely revolutionary movements emanating from below. The development of nuclear weapons encouraged the post-

Stalinist leadership in Russia to codify these tactics into the coherent policy of 'peaceful co-existence.' The Chinese, in challenging the revolutionary validity of such a policy, revived the Stalin–Trotsky controversy in a new form. The Chinese, like Trotsky, oppose in the name of revolutionary internationalism any compromise with 'imperialism.' The Yugoslavs, their most explicit critics, accuse the Chinese of confusing world revolution with a war of national conquest (which reminds us of the Jacobin dilemma) and argue that socialism can show no higher sense of international solidarity with the workers of the capitalist states than by making itself the great force for world peace.

14 Patriotism and anti-patriotism

On 12 July 1870, there appeared in Paris a manifesto issued by members of the First International: 'French, German, Spanish workmen! let our voices unite in one cry of reprobation against war!' Meetings of workers held at Chemnitz and Brunswick endorsed this resolution and the sentiment which inspired it. And yet when the Second Empire collapsed, it was the left-wing Government of National Defence which attempted to carry on the war, it was the democrat Gambetta who toured the provinces organising military resistance, it was Blanqui who declared: 'are we, with resources they (the men of 1792) never had, to perish beneath the heel of Prussia before the contemptuous smile of Europe?' The French Right had launched the war and was now the party of peace; the French Left had opposed the war and was now calling for its renewal.

Patriotism is an elusive entity because wars change their political and social content with surprising rapidity. Patriotism is not an absolute, a sentiment which a man either has or does not have, but rather a mediary between a social situation and an international one. The anarchists were convinced anti-patriots; but the Paris Commune had a federalist basis and so its patriotism became for them automatically sacrosanct. In 1904 Domela Nieuwenhuis organised an anarchist anti-militarist, anti-patriotic Congress; yet in 1914 Kropotkin wrote to Jean Grave: 'don't let these atrocious conquerors again crush latin civilisation and the French people . . .' Why this betrayal of principle? Behind Kropotkin's emotion there lay a type of logic. Was not 'latin civilisation' the only one in which anarchism had taken root, and were not 'the atrocious conquerors' – the Germans – absolutely resistant to libertarian influences?

It was a fusion of particularist instinct and artificial reasoning which swept the Socialist Parties of Europe into war in 1914. Every effort had been made to avert the catastrophe of socialists fighting socialists, workers fighting workers. At Stuttgart in 1907 the International had, in a mood of euphoria, endorsed Hervé's proposal that a declaration of war should be met by an international general strike. But in 1910, on calmer reflection, these

Domela Nieuwenhuis,
anarchist leader from Holland
and an apostle of
anti-patriotism in the
years preceding the
First World War.

plans were shelved. The Germans and Austrians admitted to themselves, if not to others, that they would be powerless against their autocratic governments. Among the French socialists, Guesde was sceptical and Jaurès was preoccupied with his plan for the substitution of popular militias for regular armies. The leaders met together at Brussels on 29 July 1914 in a final but abortive attempt to hold off the inevitable. France was allied to Russia. The SPD went crusading against the Tsar, the French and British Lefts against the Kaiser.

The German socialists are often accused of responsibility for the betrayal of 1914. This is true only in the sense that Germany was at that moment undoubtedly the aggressor nation. On the other hand, they proved themselves in the event more critical of their own government than did the French (whose President had recently returned from a state visit to the Tsar). In 1907 Karl Liebknecht's *Militarism and Anti-Militarism* had cost him eighteen months' imprisonment. On 25 July 1914, *Vorwaerts* publicly denounced the German Chancellor and the Austrians for fostering war fever. Rosa Luxemburg, who with Liebknecht and Franz Mehring had ceaselessly denounced German militarism, was prosecuted in 1914 for a speech in which she said: 'if they expect us to murder our French and other foreign brothers, then let us tell them: "No, under no circumstances!"' In the event, only fourteen of the 110 socialist deputies in the Reichstag were opposed to voting the war credits; the minority bowed to the majority. But it was in Germany, rather than in France or Britain, that the socialist tide first began to roll back towards an anti-patriotic stand. In December 1914, Liebknecht alone refused to vote the renewal of war credits; a year later twenty socialists, including Bernstein, followed suit (the anti-patriots did not coincide exactly with the revolutionaries and the patriots with the reformists, as Lenin claimed, but there was a pronounced correlation in that direction). Rosa Luxemburg was imprisoned and Liebknecht sentenced to hard labour. But the growing disenchantment with German war aims could not be checked. Hugo Haase and Kautsky published their *The Demand of the Hour*, charging the German government with having converted the war into an imperialist venture, and in 1917 the SPD finally split on the issue, a left-wing faction setting up the USPD. The 'revolution' became permanent; an even more extremist group broke with the USPD to form the Spartacus League, which was responsible for serious strikes in the Berlin munitions factories. Meanwhile, Austrian socialism travelled with greater unity towards an anti-patriotic position. In 1916 Friedrich Adler assassinated the Chancellor, Sturgkh, as a protest against the war policy, and by October 1917 the Austrian Party as a whole had reached a position corresponding to that adopted by the USPD in Germany.

The French Right attributed to the SFIO a more intransigent

'The war to end all wars.' An army recruiting centre in Britain, 1914. The attempts of international socialism to head off the outbreak of war were brushed aside by a wave of patriotism which swept through all classes in the countries concerned.

anti-patriotism than the facts warranted. Charles Maurras wrote on 18 July 1914: 'everyone knows it; M. Jaurès is Germany.' Jaurès was described in the press as the 'Kaiser's reptile.' A few days later *l'Action Française* went so far as to suggest that his assassination would not harm France. While it is true that Jaurès had in 1913 led the campaign against the extension of military service, and had denounced the collusion of the great arms cartels,

he never in fact subscribed to the fiction that the workers have no country. In the final *denouement* he became convinced not only that his own government desired peace but also that 'this Teuton diplomacy is of a brutality and hypocrisy that I would never have suspected.' The SFIO voted the war credits unanimously on the day that the assassinated Jaurès was buried. The ardent insurrectionist Gustave Hervé promptly converted his paper, *La Guerre Sociale*, into an ultra-patriotic sheet, *La Victoire*. Nor was Guesde in any sense a threat to the *Union sacrée*. Arguing that wars were symptomatic of capitalism and that to abolish the one it was first necessary to overthrow the other, he recalled witnessing the patriotism of the Parisians in 1870 and concluded, correctly, that the beginning of a war would be the least revolutionary of all situations. Opposition to the war developed more cautiously than it did within the SPD; there were no splits; it was only after the

World War I. Russian peasants in uniform advancing
to the front line at Salonika, 1916.
Two years later mass patriotism in Russia was
virtually burnt out, and the Bolsheviks
were able to conclude a humiliating peace with Germany
without losing their support.

war had ended that the SFIO proclaimed boldly that, 'it is capitalism in all countries which bears the responsibility and the eternal shame of the war.'

The anti-patriotic pretensions of the revolutionary syndicalists also collapsed like a pricked bubble in 1914. In 1902 the Congress of Bourses had refused to distinguish between wars of aggression and wars of defence, wars of oppression and wars of liberation. Six years later, the CGT adopted a motion affirming that the workers had no country, that all wars were waged against the workers and should be met by an international general strike. Griffuelhes had made an attempt in 1906 to secure the co-operation of the German unions but to no avail. The brave front was maintained to the last. On 26 July 1914, *La Bataille Syndicaliste* urged the workers to 'answer any declaration of war by a revolutionary general strike.'

But rapid conscription and the replacement of union labour by women undermined the CGT's network of authority. So seriously had the High Command taken socialist and syndicalist propaganda that it expected a desertion rate among the reservists of ten per cent; in fact it was no more than two per cent. A wave of proletarian patriotism swept all before it. Merrheim, of the Metal Workers' Federation, later explained: 'we were completely disabled, completely panic-stricken.' Throughout Europe the masses marched to the front in the name of 'justice,' 'civilisation' or 'the war to end all wars'; often the slogans were less exalted, symbols of dark prejudice and hatred.

The leaders of the Labour Party in Britain generally accepted their assigned role of keeping the working class disciplined and loyal to the cause. Arthur Henderson and others held a succession of ministerial positions under Asquith and Lloyd George. Henderson served in the war cabinet. The Marxist H. M. Hyndman, who had never concealed his hostility to Germany and her growing navy, defined the war as 'the final effort of Prussian militarism to retain its predominance at home by conquest and annexation abroad.' Ramsay MacDonald, on the other hand, who was considerably more reserved in his attitude, resigned as leader of the

Allied Conference at the British Foreign Office, July 1924.
At the left stands Frank Kellogg,
an American who worked to outlaw war.
In the centre are Herriot and MacDonald,
Premiers of France and Britain,
both of whom were opposed to the harsher type of patriotism.

Party's parliamentary group, and criticised the government; within the ILP pacifist and anti-war feeling remained strong. Among the left-wing radical intellectuals, the Union of Democratic Control represented and expressed a general suspicion of the government's real war aims and of any tampering with democratic government in the name of patriotic solidarity.

Italy entered the war in 1915 with the majority of the PSI in tow, although a minority associated themselves with Lenin's Zimmerwald movement. Among the Russians, Plekhanov was exceptional in his support for the Entente. The Russian Marxists, to their credit, did not twist logic as others had done and champion the liberties of the Russian people against the Kaiser. The Mensheviks Martov, Dan and Axelrod, together with SR leaders like M. Natanson and V. Chernov, rejected all patriotism, as did the Bolsheviks. In August 1915, Lenin described the war as being 'between two groups of predatory Great Powers, over the division of the colonies, over the enslavement of other nations, over advantages and privileges in the world market.' A year later he further elaborated this theme, explaining how the Powers had completed the seizure of the unoccupied colonial territories and how henceforward only redivision was possible. Britain had grabbed vast spheres of control, but Germany had latterly outstripped her in terms of productive power and capital resources for investment. How, asked Lenin, could such an anomaly be resolved except by war? Working through the Zimmerwald movement from Switzerland, he pressed home his attacks not only on the 'social patriots' but also on the 'Centre' factions (the USPD, the ILP and Longuet's *minoritaires* in France) who desired peace alone, and not revolution. This, in his eyes, was a diluted form of patriotism.

The case of the Second World War illustrates even more vividly that patriotism is not simply a sentiment but also a type of logic dictated by political predilections within the Right–Left antithesis. The British Labour Party, for example, had in 1933 pledged itself 'to take no part in war and to resist it with the whole force of the Labour movement . . . including a general strike.' But the Party

gradually discovered that its call for all-round disarmament was incompatible with its plea for collective security through the League of Nations. Confronted by Hitler and Mussolini, by the consequences of appeasing fascism, it began to realise also the futility of acknowledging that democracy needed weapons of defence and at the same time rejecting the Conservative government's arms programme. The anti-patriotic Party of 1933 supported the war in 1939 and joined a coalition government in 1940; the transition had been one of political logic born of changing circumstances.

The French socialists underwent a similar evolution. In 1935 Blum described the two-year military service law as 'an attempt to build up French militarism.' But with the advent of Hitler, the Spanish Civil War, the rape of Czechoslovakia, 'French militarism' had to surrender its privileged position as 'enemy-number-one' in the socialist perspective. The French Left did not become anti-German, it became vehemently anti-Nazi. But militant Nazism was represented by Germany and the Germans, just as the frontiers of democracy had been rolled back to France and Britain alone of the great European states; consequently the French Left, like the British, became 'patriotic' in the sense that the war against Nazism took of necessity a national form. There were, of course, integral pacifists like Paul Faure and Lansbury who disagreed, as did the Trotskyist doctrinaires who clung to the formula of 'revolutionary defeatism,' but the majority were open to the kind of logical evolution described.

The communist odyssey in these years also illustrates the elusive quality of patriotism. Before 1934 the communists were anti-patriots; from 1934 until 1939, patriots; from 1939 until 1941, again anti-patriots; from 1941 until 1947, the most fervent of patriots. In signing the Franco–Soviet Pact in 1935, Stalin gave his blessing to French rearmament, and the French Party thereafter denounced the policy of non-intervention in Spain and the capitulation at Munich. Even after the news of the Nazi–Soviet Pact became known, the communists continued to call for the defence of Poland and on 2 September they voted for the war credits.

Later in September a new 'logic' intervened, not a political logic natural to the situation, but rather Stalin's perennial insistence on imposing a monolithic pattern of thought and action on the whole communist movement. Word came from Moscow that the war was an 'imperialist' one and that its continuation was a matter of Anglo-French culpability. The foreign communists had to choose. In France, a majority remained loyal to the USSR and called for an immediate peace, but twenty-one of the seventy-two deputies broke with the Party. The communists claimed that the ruling class was betraying France to the point of treason, but this was a mere play on words; France was at war with Nazi Germany. Furthermore, after the German occupation of Paris the Party went to the length of approaching the military authorities for permission to publish *l'Humanité* and of celebrating in that paper the newly cemented 'friendship' between the French people and the German soldiers. But the communist strategy assumed different dimensions at different levels. The collapse of the French army can in no way be attributed to communist influence; Thorez's own desertion neither was nor was intended to be an example to the conscripted Party militants, the vast majority of whom remained with their units and many of whom were decorated for their gallantry in action.

In June 1941 Hitler launched his attack on the Soviet Union. The French communists became at once the backbone of the patriotic Resistance and set up their own militia units, the *Francs-Tireurs*, while collaborating with all forces, whatever their political colouring, who were prepared to resist Hitler and the Vichy régime. De Gaulle, previously a 'tool of the City of London' was reincarnated as a fellow patriot.

But 'patriotism' assumed perhaps its most elusive form in the course of the Italian Resistance. Italy became after 1941 a member of a coalition at war with the USSR; consequently the communists and socialists who provoked and organised the strikes in Turin and Milan in 1942–3 were objectively 'anti-patriots.' In October 1941 the CP, PSI and democratic Action Party – the backbone of the Italian Left – assumed an anti-patriotic position by demanding an immediate peace and the restoration of Italian democracy. But in 1943 Italy changed sides in the war. The left-wing partisans fighting the Germans in the North were thus transformed into 'patriots' and the strikes of March 1944 in Milan, Turin and Genoa were likewise patriotic strikes. But the objective role and the subjective intention need not correspond exactly. The Italian Resistance did indeed wish to expel the Germans, but its attitude nevertheless differed on certain fundamentals from that of the Badoglio government and the Allies. The latter were concerned simply with the defeat of Germany; the Resistance fighters saw themselves as engaged in a civil war against native fascism, a revolutionary struggle to ensure the republican and democratic character of the post-war régime.

In Greece, the German occupation signified the substitution of one fascist régime for another, a factor which led the Right, the supporters of Metaxas' pre-war government, to the conclusion that they had much to gain and little to lose from a quiet life, while the Left, and particularly the communists and their sympathisers, became the backbone of the military Resistance. British officers on missions to Greece unanimously praised the role of ELAS, the fighting forces representing the communist-dominated National Liberation Front (EAM). But with the withdrawal of German forces and the arrival of British troops, the contradiction between the subjective attitude of ELAS and their objective utility to the Allied war effort came into the open and was resolved only by a civil war which led to the return of the Right, assisted by Anglo-American forces, to power.

Perhaps the most remarkable of the patriotic Resistance movements under communist leadership was that which took shape in Yugoslavia. Tito's partisans embarked upon a triple enterprise: to fight the Germans, to defeat the collaborators, and, through a 'Risorgimento' founded on a common social and patriotic passion, to prevent Yugoslavia from disintegrating into its ethnic and religious components. Here again the political ambiguities of 'patriotism' were fully in evidence. The royalist General Mihailovitch was in a sense a patriot; he hoped that the Western Allies would restore Yugoslav independence. But, faced with an immediate choice between the Germans and Italians on the one hand and native communism on the other, he felt compelled by his social and political beliefs to throw in his lot with the Germans and Italians. His chetnik forces took part in the fourth German offensive against Tito.

Still in the realm of ambiguity, we may conclude by examining briefly the realignments dictated by the onset of the Cold War. The communists, there can be no doubt, are attached to their native France or their native Italy by bonds of sentiment no less strong than those which bind the Right. According to the communists, the upper classes sold out the national domain to American finance; according to their opponents, the communists are themselves lackeys of a foreign power. Thorez declared that Frenchmen would never fight the Soviet Union, and in February 1949 Togliatti followed him in affirming that if Soviet troops pursued an 'aggressor' on to Italian soil, it would be the duty of the popular masses to support them. If the communists are at present 'anti-patriots,' it can be for one reason only – the majority of their fellow-countrymen regard the presence of American troops as a protection and not an occupation.

PART FIVE

Sociology of the Left

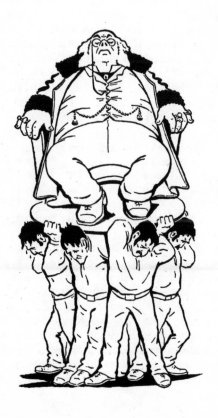

15 Social class and social status

Marx never fully and finally defined a social class, but it is quite clear that he regarded the basic factors as being the relationship to the means of production and to the employment of labour. Alain Touraine is probably correct in regarding classes as 'groups defined by their place in the social process of production.' But this, as he realises, and as Marx realised also, is not enough. Classes, Touraine points out, are in addition elements in a system of opposites. In *The German Ideology*, Marx stressed that individuals only form a class when they wage a common struggle against another class. (Stalin's claim for the existence of 'non-antagonistic classes' in the USSR is meaningless; where there are classes there are conflicts.)

We now have two component elements of a social class: its place in the social process of production and its place in a particular system of opposites. But even this is not enough. The duke's tenants may fulfil both these stipulations, yet they may also be sympathetic to his political aspirations and entertain no desire to upset the *status quo*. They lack class consciousness. Marx wrote:

> In so far as millions of families live under economic conditions of existence that divide their mode of life, their interests and their culture from those of other classes, and put them in a hostile contrast to the latter, they form a class. In so far as there is merely a local interconnection among the small peasants, and the identity of their interests begets no unity, no national union and no political organisation, they do not form a class.

A class, in short, must become aware of its homogeneity and its conflict with other classes. How rapidly this consciousness will develop it is difficult to be sure. Lenin argued that full political class consciousness could be brought to the proletariat only from without, and Bukharin observed in the same vein that, 'a class discharging a definite function in the process of production may already exist as an aggregate of persons before it exists as a self-conscious class; we have a class [*sic*] but no class consciousness.'

Obviously class antagonisms constantly alter their form with the evolution of the system of production. The evidence suggests that class consciousness assumes its most coherent and politically effective form by reducing the complex stresses and strains within an elaborate organism to a simple and dichotomic view of society as being divided between the rulers and the ruled, the rich and the poor, those for whom others work and those who work for others, as the case may be. 'Long live the Third Estate!' became an emotive rallying cry in the first months of the French revolution, a slogan which suggested by implication a direct struggle between the majority and a privileged minority. Babeuf describes social conflict in terms of a war between the great mass of the nation, the producers, and a handful of exploiters, the 'speculators and merchants . . .'. It is significant in this connection that the *Communist Manifesto* not only predicted that society would progressively gravitate into two camps, eliminating the intermediate strata, but also that the revolution would materialise only after it had done so.

Society, however, did not gravitate into two great camps; on the contrary, it became increasingly complex and diversified. Engels and Lenin began to complain about the political conservatism of the 'workers' aristocracy,' a phenomenon which draws attention to the factor which Marx failed to take into consideration – social status. As an explanation for the totality of political behaviour, the class consideration proves to be inadequate and unduly schematic. Hence the importance of introducing into the analysis the question of status, as defined by such criteria as birth, education, income, wealth and power – by factors which, like class ones, have an objective existence and are reproduced subjectively in terms of social and political consciousness. It is with this subjectivity that we are concerned. It must, however, be pointed out that status criteria enjoy only a transitorily objective existence, whereas class criteria are permanently objective; in other words, birth, wealth, etc., represent different values to the individual and to society in general in different environments. Thus in Britain aristocratic birth counts for more than in the USA or USSR, and income for less than in the USA. Nevertheless, a fairly uniform valuation has been attached to the principal status factors in modern Europe, and they have tended to affect the individual's class and political sympathies according to a discernible pattern.

Briefly, some of the more important of the operative status factors should be pointed out. Education is, in general, a left-orientated status factor in the sense that the best-educated elements in each social class are inclined to show the greatest proletarian class consciousness or sympathy for the proletariat. A high standard of living, on the contrary, tends to produce rightist sympathies. Where a higher education has been responsible for a higher standard of living, the outcome is variable. Regional and ethnic factors also affect class consciousness and political allegiances; anarchism took root in Catalonia, with its ancient hostility to Castilian centralism, and the British CP derived much of its initial support from Scotland, South Wales and Ireland – areas with a tradition of fierce Anglophobia. Later, the Party gathered a following among the Jews of London. Jews have, in fact, been prominent in the socialist movement throughout Europe. Marx and Lassalle were Jews, as were Bernstein, Rosa Luxemburg, Kurt Eisner, the Adlers, Trotsky, Radek and Blum. Approximately one SPD deputy out of nine in the pre-1914 Reichstag was a Jew.

Women have proved themselves to be marginally more conservative than men. Similarly, the old are more conservative than the young. The latter lack social integration (an important status factor), as do miners, fishermen, sailors, longshoremen and forestry workers – all of whom are inclined to adopt a more radical attitude than comparable proletarian groups.

It is not surprising that time and again left-wing movements have drawn not only their theorists but also their leaders from the ranks of the intelligentsia, a group which combines a high educational level with a relative lack of social integration. In the last quarter of the nineteenth century, John Allemane was the only one of the notable socialist leaders in France to have come from a proletarian background. Bebel's humble origins were exceptional among the leaders of the SPD. Of the thirty-two socialist deputies in the Rome parliament in 1900, twenty-eight were university graduates. The Bolshevik Council of People's Commissars consisted in 1917 of eleven intellectuals and four workers. The leading names of the Comintern in its early years were those of intellectuals; Gramsci, Togliatti, Levi, Frossard, Souvarine, Smernal, Roland-Holst, Gorter and Markovitch. It was one of Stalin's 'achievements' to have reversed this social balance both inside and outside Russia.

With these general considerations in mind, we may examine in turn the political records of the principal social classes.

16 The Left and social classes

The 'bourgeoisie' is a class; the 'middle class,' paradoxically, is not. The term 'bourgeoisie' refers to those who own the means of production (generally industrial) and who control finance capital, and whose attitude towards the wage-earning class is in consequence one of overt or latent antagonism. The 'middle class' is, in terms both of its structure and of its political behaviour, a more complicated phenomenon. Its members share in common no single relationship to the means of production; they include petit-bourgeois owners and employers, professional men working independently, and salaried officials, employees, teachers and so forth. Their only unity is as a status group in the 'upper-middle-lower' status hierarchy, a status group to which we have come by misleading usage to attach the name of 'class.' The middle class rarely achieves any coherent class consciousness. Its primary antagonisms and sympathies vary according to the immediate situation; in the 1840's it shared the workers' hostility to the industrial and financial bourgeoisie, but in June 1848 it shared the latter's fear of the workers. The middle class has, despite lapses into fascism in times of crisis, tended towards the moderate Left, towards Jacobinism or Benthamite radicalism. The new middle class, clerks, functionaries, technicians – all salaried workers but separated from the proletariat by status factors – has in recent times gravitated towards the Radical Party or towards moderate socialism. It looks now to the state to steer a course between the claims of big business and those of organised labour.

The rapid industrialisation of Europe in the course of the nineteenth century threw a particular strain on the independent artisans and craftsmen, a petit-bourgeois class separated from the proletariat by its ownership of its own productive tools and from the bourgeoisie proper by its slender capital resources, its inability to employ more than one or two assistants and by its losing battle with technological change and the development of large-scale industry. The social threat came from above; the artisans and craftsmen moved to the Left, only later parting company with the proletariat when its political aspirations began to assume a socialist form. In Germany, it was not so much the workers as the handi-craftsmen who were the dynamic revolutionary force in 1848. Under the Second Empire political class consciousness was at its most intense among the more or less independent artisans working in small *ateliers* and dreading the day when mechanisation would relieve them of a livelihood. Of the mutualist leaders in France, Tolain was a carver, Limousin a lace machinist, Fribourg an en-graver and Varlin a bookbinder. Anarchism took root in Lyons, a town of silk weavers, carpenters and shoemakers, and also among the watchmakers of the Jura.

Leaving aside the exceptional case of Britain, the most formid-able left-wing social force in the early nineteenth century issued from the spontaneous collaboration of sections of the petit-bourgeoisie with the nascent proletariat. Although the *sans-culottes* were not strictly a class, they achieved a type of cohesive consciousness based on a common social antagonism which approximated to class consciousness. The Parisian *sans-culottes* contained, besides wage-earners, workshop masters, craftsmen, small shopkeepers and domestics. In the armed attacks on the Bastille and the Tuileries, and in the Champ de Mars demonstra-tion, the small shopkeepers and workshop masters threw their employees, journeymen and apprentices into the fray. By degrees they supported increasingly radical and democratic programmes; encouraged and guided by the *Enragés* and the Hébertists, they co-dified their economic demands in the shape of the *Maximum Générale* which they imposed for a time on the Jacobin Conven-tion. Politically an *avant-garde* and economically an *arrière-garde*, defending blindly the traditional economy against the jungle law of emergent capitalism, they were interested in taxing the rich, keeping prices down, extracting guarantees of work and public education, and securing assistance for the sick and aged. Even the proletarian element in the *sans-culottes* knew little as yet of socialism.

The unity of the *sans-culottes* was political and therefore episo-dic. The participants of the '*trois glorieuses*' of July 1830, when the Bourbon monarchy was overthrown, were similar in social com-

Communist workers in Milan demonstrate against the killing of
six workers in Modena by police, January 1950.

position to the captors of the Bastille. Again in 1848 masters and
journeymen marched together. The leaders of the left-wing republican movement in Rome in 1849 included publicans, soldiers,
cobblers, hatters, carters, joiners, office workers, butchers, painters,
teachers and students. The Parisian 'city mob' had blazed the trail
to the Left. In the 1790's the Viennese 'mob' was loyalist and anti-
Jacobin; by 1848 it was left-wing and revolutionary.

It was in Britain that the industrial proletariat first assumed size
and shape. In the period 1801–41, the population of London more
than doubled while those of Manchester and Liverpool more than
trebled. The first reaction of the workers to exploitation and
sweated labour did not always take a political form and was on
more than one occasion channelled into the suicidal activity of
machine-breaking. In March 1831 a wave of machine-breaking
spread across France from Saint-Etienne to Bordeaux, Paris and

The British upper strata mobilise against the social peril.
A special mounted force during the General Strike of 1926.

233

Lyons. The rising at Lyons in November, which fused all the workers' demands and which attracted international attention, was purely socio-economic and without political direction. By 1834, however, the *Société des droits de l'homme* had made its influence felt in the proletarian quarters of Paris and Lyons. The workers became increasingly aware of the fortunes being made by capitalists and by speculators on the Bourse, and as they did so their incoherent rage was moulded into a coherent antagonism. In the June days of 1848 the strictly proletarian element among the rioting *sans-culottes* was higher than on any previous *journée*.

The Socialist Parties of the Second International drew their strength from the great provincial industrial concentrations, from the Nord, the Pas-de-Calais, Central Germany, Wales, the British Midlands, Piedmont and Lombardy. Revolutions and attempted revolutions continued to take place in capital cities (in 1920 the

Italian workers were fatally weakened by their lack of strength in Rome) but, as the Paris Commune showed, command of the capital alone was not enough. The British Labour Party initially drew its rank and file almost exclusively from the industrial proletariat; forty-two per cent of the Italian Party's membership consisted of urban workers, and over eighty per cent of the German Party's.

The most perplexing problems about proletarian class consciousness and political affiliation are these: why is the working class as a whole more left-wing, more extremist, in one country than in another? when are skilled workers more left-wing than unskilled, and vice versa? To these questions no entirely satisfactory answer can be found.

In those European nations where the average income-per-head is low, the working class tends to be politically more extremist. This is not so much because proletarian living standards are lower in absolute terms than those in wealthier countries, but because in the poorer nations they are lower *in comparison to those of the upper classes*. This greater inequality breeds greater extremism and corruption among the possessing classes, thus further stimulating working-class intransigence. In Britain, where income-per-head was abnormally high, H. M. Hyndman complained in 1901: 'I fail to detect among the English workers that class consciousness and class antagonism without which no good can ever be done.' In Catalonia, where living standards were abnormally low and social inequalities much more pronounced, the workers were attracted by a revolutionary doctrine, anarcho-syndicalism. The British workers became more class conscious and violent in the years immediately preceding the First World War when social inequalities were at their most ostentatious.

It is also the case that rapidity of industrial change (and therefore of social dislocation) breeds extremism and that this rapidity frequently occurs in backward economies hastening to close the gap. In its earliest and most rapid phase, British industrialisation bred Chartism. In Russia, industrialisation was imposed with great speed in the period 1880–1914, the result being that the workers

lent themselves to Marxist leadership. In Germany, the more moderate sections of the SPD were based on the more stable industries, and vice versa; the sudden acceleration of industrial development in Sweden from 1900 until 1919 led to a growth of extremism in the unions and the Party, whereas the more measured pace of development in Denmark encouraged moderation.

With regard to the second problem, that of the skilled as opposed to the unskilled workers, we find that in general the former are more conservative, more content, than the latter. Before illustrating this point, two reservations must be made. In its early stages of development, a working-class movement is likely to derive its leadership from the skilled strata. They are organised and unionised, whereas the unskilled are as yet not. The superior bargaining position of the skilled reinforces their militancy and their courage, whereas the unskilled worker knows how easily he can be replaced by another. The skilled workers are better educated – a left-orientated status factor. The earliest trade unions in Britain were formed by printers, hatters and tailors, and until 1840 Chartism derived its main impetus from the upper levels of the working class. In France it was the skilled workers who tended to embark upon strike action rather than the absolutely pauperised textile workers. The first German communists (intellectuals apart) were either artisans or skilled workers.

The second reservation concerns the attitude of the unskilled workers and of the casual, non-unionised labour known as the lumpenproletariat. The *Communist Manifesto* referred to 'the "dangerous class," the social scum, that passively rotting mass thrown off by the lowest layers of the old society' as being the most likely to become 'a bribed tool of reactionary intrigue.' Three years later Marx denounced the lumpenproletariat for having lent itself to Louis Bonaparte's counter-revolutionary Society of 10 December. In subsequent decades the lowest stratum of workers came to be regarded with contempt by organised labour and were known as *Streikbrecher* in Germany, *krumiri* in Italy, blacklegs or scabs in Britain, *jaunes*, *renards* or *bedouins* in France. In illustrating the comparative conservatism of skilled workers, we often have to rely on surveys which limit themselves to a simple division of the proletariat into skilled and unskilled; in a sense this can be misleading, since a triple distinction between skilled, semi-skilled and unskilled sometimes reveals a leftwards orienation in the following order: semi-skilled, unskilled, skilled.

Under the impact of the long mid-Victorian era of prosperity, the skilled workers in Britain abandoned their early militancy and contented themselves with pressing their sectional interests through the unions and the Liberal Party. In 1892 Engels conceded that the 'workers' aristocracy', the mechanics, carpenters and building workers, were content with the system, and it was conspicuously the new unions rather than the old which agitated for an independent Labour Party. In the 1950's, the unskilled workers continued

The Millionaires (1925) by George Grosz.
Left-wing millionaires are not unknown.

to rally to the Party more strongly than the skilled. Even in Russia, where the working class as a whole was separated by a high barrier from the upper classes, the highly skilled workers found enough compensatory status factors to make Menshevism rather than Bolshevism attractive. The Bolsheviks were forced to look instead to the unskilled labour of the new industries and of the textile factories.

In the present century a further pattern of allegiance has emerged. Where the extremist faction, whether it be communist or revolutionary syndicalist, is small it attracts the skilled workers; where it is large, as in France, Italy, Spain or Finland, the unskilled workers and the lower-income groups. Statistics compiled in 1951 indicate that in France eighteen per cent of the above-average workers, forty per cent of the average workers and forty-five per cent of the poorer workers supported the CP; whereas forty-one per cent of the above-average, twenty-seven per cent of the average and twenty-two per cent of the poorer workers supported the moderate SFIO. In Italy also, the poor, average and above-average workers supported the Communist Party in that order of priority, although support for the left-wing Nenni socialists followed the semi-skilled, unskilled, skilled pattern. Obviously the higher strata are deflected from extremism by their superior status, conditions of work and standard of living.

Where, on the contrary, the extreme Left is relatively small, as in Britain, the appeal it exercises is confined mainly to skilled workers. Here two status factors relevant to the skilled workers, higher income and superior education, affect individual workers in opposite ways. The majority of skilled workers find in their relative affluence cause to waver in their allegiance to the Labour Party itself, while a small minority from their ranks convert their educational and technical training into an acute class consciousness and impatience with the 'apathy' of the majority; this drives them towards the Communist Party. A similar complex of conflicting impulses may help to account for the situation in pre-1914 France when skilled workers simultaneously reinforced the reformist trend within the SFIO and provided the hard core of the CGT's militant élite. But an additional circumstance distinguishes France in 1900 from Britain in 1950; in the former many of the skilled workers employed in small productive units were still resisting mentally and physically the challenge of large-scale industry, the assembly-line technique and the Taylor system. Not only did the influx of peasants into the towns threaten their standard of living and the indispensability of their specialised skills, but the employing class itself, the bourgeoisie, afforded by its intransigence no opportunity for compromising with the capitalist system. A large proportion of the skilled workers accordingly took refuge in a militant class consciousness and in an ideology aiming to over-throw the system *en bloc*.

Cutting across the patterns so far outlined is a further considera-tion. Any single occupational category of worker tends to be more left-wing when located in a large city and a large plant than when employed in a smaller unit of work and habitation. Large concen-trations not only stimulate a sense of class comradeship, they also enable the unions and the party to exercise a more penetrating influence. Under the Weimar Republic the communist workers were to be found in the industrial concentrations of Berlin-Brandenburg, Halle-Merseburg, Hamburg and the Rhineland. The French Communist Party planted its roots among the proletarians of the Parisian industrial suburbs, the industrial concentrations of the North-East and the mining areas of the North. Similarly, it is over the factories of the great urban centres of Piedmont and Lombardy that the red flag flies. Here the skilled workers drawing large pay packets are as likely as not to champion the CP, although their aspirations may be very far from revolutionary.

The peasantry as an entity cannot be regarded as a class unless we define a class by its working relationship to a particular means of production (the land) rather than by its relationship to the social process of production as a whole (capitalism). The wealthy peasant owning land and hiring labourers (the British 'farmer') is a rural bourgeois; the landless labourer is likewise a rural proletarian.

Rarely do the peasants assume an independent, still less a lead-ing, political role. Depending on the situation, they follow the aristocracy, the bourgeoisie or, occcasionally, the proletariat. Most peasant movements before 1848 were conservative in emphasis and rallied to the banner of 'priest and king.' This applies to the peasants of southern Italy in 1799, the Carlist guerrillas who fought the Spanish liberals in the 1830's and 1840's, the peasants who swelled the ranks of the monarchist armies in 1848 and those who turned in France to Louis Bonaparte. The populist evangelists of the

SOCIALISM

PROSPERITY

THROTTLING THE COUNTRY

1870's were constantly denounced and betrayed by the Russian peasants themselves who remained, despite their heavy burdens, stubbornly loyal to the Tsar and his church. The Commune evoked no sympathy in the rural provinces of France.

In what circumstances, then, have peasants thrown in their lot with the Left? Land-hunger is a primary motive; the close proximity of poor and wealthy farmers excites discontent; thirdly, peasants gravitate to the Left in regions having an ingrained hostility towards and desire for independence from the central government.

The French peasants benefited from the distribution of the great estates at the time of the revolution. In certain areas the poorer peasants, like the *sans-culottes* with whom they shared an anti-bourgeois (but not socialist) outlook, were prepared to follow the Jacobins beyond the first, bourgeois revolution. In Italy, where property distribution was exceptionally inegalitarian and where in 1900 ninety per cent of the proprietors (i.e. the peasants) possessed only fourteen per cent of the available land, the landless labourers were driven into the Socialist Party. The South, where tension was most acute, seemed beyond reform. The CP's share of the total vote in that region rose from twenty-one to thirty per cent in the period 1946–53, conversions being most noticeable among the very poor, the landless labourers.

Secondly, the close proximity of poor and wealthy farmers, the provocation of visibly acute inequalities, also breeds radicalism. In 1848–9, the Montagnard platform found support in the Bourbonnais, where the crop-sharing system was resented, and after 1936 the PCF made considerable gains in the same area. In Sicily, too, the poor could never forget the existence of the rich. Resentment produced a remarkably coherent response in the shape of the Fasci, peasant organisations aiming to elect socialist provincial councillors and parliamentary deputies. At Piana, in the latifundist grain-growing uplands, the local council was socialist by 1914 and later communist. In subsequent decades, particularly after the Second World War, the CP prospered in the areas of Central Italy where poor and wealthy farmers existed side by side, in the Po

Valley, in South Tuscany and around Bologna, Ferrara, Ravenna and Forli.

It was not absolute poverty which fostered a radical (anarchist) spirit among the peasants of southern Spain, but rather the appearance of the disturbing inequalities which followed the sale of civil and ecclesiastical property on the open market and the introduction of capitalist social and legal relationships in the countryside. Violence flared up periodically but regularly in the districts where vast estates and small plots existed in close proximity. Large estates, absentee landlords, fixed rents, high rates of interest – this was the soil in which rural anarchism flowered in Spain. Yet the fact that Italian peasants took to Marxism and the Spanish to anarchism may be attributed to an accident of chronology; whereas in the 1870's Bakuninism could make little headway against Bourbonism, Catholicism, Garibaldianism, the Mafia and other deep-rooted forces in southern Italy, in Spain, by way of contrast, Bakuninism filled an ideological vacuum. Later, when the influence of the traditional cults began to wane in Italy, it was Marxism which stood poised to replace them.

In France no less than in Spain, the peasants were inclined to jettison their inherent conservatism in regions harbouring hostility towards the 'system' as incarnated by the capital city with its parasites and corrupt politicians. The French Communist Party has flourished in areas almost identical to those which were Montagnard a century earlier. In November 1946 the Party polled one-third of the vote in twenty-three departments south of the Loire, the most considerable concentration consisting of eleven contiguous departments on the northern and western slopes of the Massif Central, merging with the Garonne valley. The Mediterranean littoral can be regarded as another red belt. In such areas the Party's principal attraction is not usually ideological; aware of peasant aversion to collectivisation, it wisely relies on the ambiguous slogan, 'the land to those who work it.' What communism represents to these peasants is protest, opposition, an intransigent refusal to compromise with the 'system.'

References

The following references are confined to recent secondary works cited in Part One

1 *The Unservile State: Essays in Liberty and Welfare*, ed. G. Watson, London, 1955, p. 25.
2 R. Graves and A. Hodge, *The Long Week-end*, London, 1950, pp. 307, 330, 331.
3 J. L. Talmon, *The Origins of Totalitarian Democracy*, London (Mercury), 1961, p. 7.
4 E. H. Carr, *The Twenty Years' Crisis, 1919–39*, London, 1939, p. 26.
5 D. Mascolo, 'Sur le Sens et l'Usage du Mot "Gauche",' *Les Temps Modernes*, 112–113, 1955, p. 1684.
6 W. G. Runciman, *Social Science and Political Theory*, Cambridge, 1963, p. 148.
7 P. Johnson, 'A Sense of Outrage', *Conviction*, London, 1959, p. 202.
8 Quoted in R. Aron, *The Opium of the Intellectuals*, trans. by T. Kilmartin, London, 1957, p. 33.
9 C. Lanzmann, 'L'Homme de Gauche,' *Les Temps Modernes*, 112–113, 1955, p. 1628.
10 G. Orwell, *Collected Essays*, London, 1961, p. 429.
11 Quoted in S. M. Lipset, *Political Man*, London (Mercury), 1963, p. 222.
12 Runciman, *op. cit.*, p. 149.
13 Lipset, *op. cit.*, p. 173.
14 Runciman, *op. cit.*, p. 151.
15 *Ibid.*, p. 146.
16 A. Thibaudet, *Les Idées Politiques de la France*, Paris, 1932, p. 9, and F. Goguel, *La Politique des Partis sous la Troisième République*, Paris, 1958, p. 547.
17 G. D. H. Cole, *Marxism and Anarchism, 1850–90*, London, 1954, p. 92.
18 G. Woodcock, *Anarchism*, Cleveland, 1962, p. 33.

Short bibliography

General

G. D. H. Cole, *A History of Socialist Thought, 1789–1939*, 5 vols, London, 1953–60. C. Landauer, *European Socialism*, 2 vols, Berkeley, 1959. R. W. Postgate, *Revolution 1789 to 1906*, London, 1920. J. L. Talmon, *The Origins of Totalitarian Democracy*, London, 1952, and *Political Messianism: the Romantic Phase*, London, 1960. E. J. Hobsbawm, *The Age of Revolution, 1789–1848*, London, 1962. E. H. Carr, *Studies in Revolution*, London, 1950. G. Lichteim, *Marxism*, London, 1961.

Topics

The French Revolution

G. Lefebvre, *The French Revolution*, 2 vols, London 1962 and 1964. J. M. Thompson, *The French Revolution*, Oxford, 1943. E. Thompson, *Popular Sovereignty and the French Constituent Assembly, 1789–1791*, Manchester, 1952. G. Rudé, *The Crowd in the French Revolution*, Oxford, 1959. A. Soboul, *The Parisian Sans-Culottes in the French Revolution*, London, 1964. A. Cobban, *The Social Interpretation of the French Revolution*, London, 1964.

The Revolutions of 1848

The Opening of an Era: 1848, ed. F. Fejtö, London, 1948. A. Soboul, *The French Revolution of 1848*, London, 1948. P. Robertson, *The Revolutions of 1848 – A Social History*, Princeton, 1952.

The Second International

J. Joll, *The Second International, 1889–1914*, London, 1955. M. M. Drachovitch, *Les Socialismes français et allemand et le problème de la guerre, 1870–1914*, Geneva, 1953, and *De Karl Marx à Léon Blum*, Geneva, 1954.

European Communism

O. Gankin and H. Fisher, *The Bolsheviks and the World War*, Stanford, 1940. D. Caute, *Communism and the French Intellectuals, 1914–60*, London, 1964. F. Borkenau, *The Communist International*,

London, 1937, and *European Communism*, London, 1953. *Communism in Western Europe*, ed. M. Einaudi, Ithaca, 1951. R. Fischer, *Stalin and German Communism*, London, 1948. H. Pelling, *The British Communist Party*, London, 1958. G. Walter, *Histoire du Parti Communiste Français*, Paris, 1948. B. Lazitch, *Les Partis Communistes d'Europe, 1919–55*, Paris, 1956. J. Fauvet, *Histoire du Parti Communiste Français, I*, Paris, 1964. *The Anti-Stalin Campaign and International Communism*, New York, 1956.

Anarchism

G. Woodcock, *Anarchism*, Cleveland, 1962. J. Maitron, *Histoire du Mouvement Anarchiste en France, 1880–1914*, Paris, 1951. J. Joll, *The Anarchists*, London, 1964.

Labour Unions and Syndicalism

A. Aspinall, *The Early English Trade Unions*, London, 1949. E. Dolléans, *Histoire du Mouvement Ouvrier, 1830–1953*, 3 vols, Paris, 1953. V. R. Lorwin, *The French Labor Movement*, Cambridge, Mass., 1954. G. D. H. Cole, *The World of Labour*, London, 1928. P. Louis, *Histoire du Mouvement Syndical en France, 1789–1948*, 2 vols, Paris, 1947–8. H. Clegg, A. Fox and A. F. Thompson, *A History of British Trade Unionism since 1889*, Vol I, Oxford, 1964.

Countries

France

J. Plamenatz, *The Revolutionary Movement in France, 1815–71*, London, 1952. E. S. Mason, *The Paris Commune*, New York, 1930. J. T. Marcus, *French Socialism in the Crisis Years, 1933–6*, New York, 1958. C. A. Micaud, *Communism and the French Left*, London, 1963. D. Ligou, *Histoire du Socialisme en France, 1871–1961*, Paris, 1962.

Great Britain

E. P. Thompson, *The Making of the English Working Class*, London, 1964. M. Beer, *A History of British Socialism*, London, 1948. M. Hovell, *The Chartist Movement*, Manchester, 1918. H. Pelling,

A Short History of the Labour Party, London, 1961. R. Miliband, *Parliamentary Socialism*, London, 1961. C. Tsuzuki, *H. M. Hyndman and British Socialism*, London, 1961. M. Cole, *The Story of Fabian Socialism*, London, 1961.

Germany and Italy

P. Gay, *The Dilemma of Democratic Socialism*, New York, 1952. W. Hilton Young, *The Italian Left*, London, 1949. R. Hostetter, *The Italian Socialist Movement. 1: Origins, 1860–82*, New York, 1958. D. Mack Smith, *Garibaldi*, London, 1954. R. P. Morgan, *German Social Democrats in the First International, 1864-72*, Cambridge, 1964. E. J. Hobsbawm, *Primitive Rebels*, Manchester, 1959.

Spain, Sweden and Russia (pre-1917)

G. Brenan, *The Spanish Labyrinth*, Cambridge, 1943. H. Thomas, *The Spanish Civil War*, London, 1961. D. C. Cattell, *Communism and the Spanish Civil War*, Berkeley, 1955. G. Orwell, *Homage to Catalonia*, London, 1951. M. W. Childs, *Sweden – the Middle Way*, New Haven, 1947. R. Fusilier, *Le Parti Socialiste Suédois*, Paris, 1954. F. Venturi, *Roots of Revolution*, London, 1960. E. Wilson, *To the Finland Station*, New York, 1940. B. Wolfe, *Three who made a Revolution*, Boston, 1960.

Soviet Union and Eastern Europe

E. H. Carr, *A History of Soviet Russia*, London, 1953–19—. I. Deutscher, *Trotsky*, 3 vols, London, 1954, 1959 and 1964, and *Stalin*, London, 1949. M. Fainsod, *How Russia is Ruled*, Cambridge, Mass., 1956. L. Schapiro, *The Communist Party of the Soviet Union*, London, 1960. A. Nove, *The Soviet Economy*, London, 1961. F. Fejtö, *Histoire des Démocraties Populaires*, Paris, 1952. H. Seton-Watson, *The East European Revolution*, London, 1950. H. Ripka, *Eastern Europe and the Post-War World*, London, 1961. A. Ulam, *Titoism and the Cominform*, Cambridge, Mass., 1962. F. A. Váli, *Rift and Revolt in Hungary*, Cambridge, Mass., 1961. V. Dedijer, *Tito Speaks*, London, 1953.

Acknowledgments

I am very grateful to my friends Mr Angus MacIntyre and Mr Gordon Phillips, who were kind enough to subject the text to searching criticisms.

I would also like to thank Mrs Enid Radcliffe and Illustration Research Service for collecting a number of the illustrations used.

Acknowledgment is due to the following for the illustrations (the number refers to the page on which the illustration appears). 2, 7, 136, 154, 235 James Klugmann Collection, photos Macdonald; 8 photo Bulloz; 10, 24, 27, 37, 39, 56, 61, 76, 83, 87, 91, 97, 113, 115, 130, 131, 134, 139, 157, 158, 165, 184, 194, 200 Radio Times Hulton Picture Library; 125, 153, 225, 228 British Museum; 17 Photographie Giraudon; 22, 96, 150, 162, 177, 179, 186, 195 Paul Popper Ltd; 29, 193 Novosti Press Agency (A. P. N.); 40, 144 photo Documentation Française; 45 The Fogg Art Museum, Harvard University; 47, 49, 74, 76, 170 The Mansell Collection; 54, 55, 64, 209 Marx Memorial Library, photo Macdonald; 56 Franco Petazzi; 70, 101, 210, 232 Keystone Press Agency Ltd; 71 Black Star Pictures; 82, 141 Historisches Bildarchiv Handke-Bud Berneck; 94 Black Star, photo Kurt Neher; 95, 217, 221 Mirrorpic; 98, 102 Fox Photos Ltd; 110 Communist Party of Great Britain; 116 S.P.A.D.E.M.; 120 Black Star, photo Paul Pietzsch; 127 *Punch*; 129, 175, 218 Camera Press Ltd; 142 National Film Archive; 143 Walter Poppel; 147 Amalgamated Engineering Union; 150 *Daily Worker*; 154 Arnoldo Mondadori Editore; 169 Popper-Handke Collection; 198 The Swedish Institute; 203 F. G. Hutchins Collection; 205 Scala; 215 C.P.L.I.-Amsterdam; 233 Central Press Ltd; 237 Marlborough Fine Art Ltd.

D. C.

Index

249

250

252

254

World University Library

Some books published or in preparation

Economics and Social Studies

The World Cities
Peter Hall, *London*

The Economics of Underdeveloped Countries
Jagdish Bhagwati, *Delhi*

Development Planning
Jan Tinbergen, *Rotterdam*

Leadership in New Nations
T. B. Bottomore, *Vancouver*

Key Issues in Criminology
Roger Hood, *Durham*

The Sociology of Communication
J. L. Aranguren, *Madrid*

Education in the Modern World
John Vaizey, *Oxford*

History

Ancient Egypt
Werner Kaiser, *Berlin*

The Emergence of Greek Democracy
W. G. Forrest, *Oxford*

Mahomet and the Great Arabian Conquests
Francesco Gabrieli, *Rome*

The Crusades
G. Widengren, *Uppsala*

The Medieval Economy
Georges Duby, *Aix-en-Provence*

The Ottoman Empire
Halil Inalcik, *Ankara*

The Rise of Toleration
Henry Kamen, *Edinburgh*

The Left in Europe
David Caute, *Oxford*

Chinese Communism
Robert C. North, *Stanford*

History and Sociology of Religion

History of the Christian Church
W. O. Chadwick, *Cambridge*

Monasticism
Dom David Knowles, *London*

Judaism
Rabbi J. Soetendorp, *Amsterdam*

The Modern Papacy
K. O. von Aretin, *Göttingen*

Sects
Bryan. Wilson, *Oxford*

Language and Literature

A Model of Language
E. M. Uhlenbeck, *Leyden*

French Literature
Raymond Picard, *Sorbonne*

Russian Literature
Ronald Hingley, *Oxford*

Satire
Matthew Hodgart, *Sussex*

The Arts

Primitive Art
Eike Haberland, *Mainz*

The Language of Modern Art
Ulf Linde, *Stockholm*

Aesthetic Theories since 1850
J. F. Revel, *Paris*

Art Nouveau
S. T. Madsen, *Oslo*

Academic Painting
Gerald Ackerman, *Stanford*

Palaeolithic Art
P. J. Ucko and A. Rosenfeld, *London*

Modern Drama
Peter Szondi, *Göttingen*

Psychology and Human Biology

Eye and Brain
R. L. Gregory, *Cambridge*

The Ear and the Brain
Edward Carterette, *U.C.L.A.*

The Variety of Man
J. P. Garlick, *London*

The Biology of Work
O. G. Edholm, *London*

Bioengineering
H. S. Wolff, *London*

Psychoses
H. J. Bochnik, *Hamburg*

Child Development
Philippe Muller, *Neuchâtel*

Man and Disease
Gernot Rath, *Göttingen*

Zoology and Botany

Animal Communication
N. Tinbergen and J. M. Cullen, *Oxford*

Mimicry
Wolfgang Wickler, *Starnberg*

Migration
Gustaf Rudebeck, *Stockholm*

The World of an Insect
Remy Chauvin, *Sorbonne*

Biological Rhythms
Janet Harker, *Cambridge*

Lower Animals
Martin Wells, *Cambridge*

Physical Science and Mathematics

Mathematics in Science and Daily Life
H. Freudenthal, *Utrecht*

The Physics of Low Temperatures
K. A. G. Mendelssohn, *Oxford*

Particles and Accelerators
Robert Gouiran, *C.E.R.N., Geneva*

Optics
A. C. S. van Heel, *Delft*

Waves and Corpuscles
J. A. E. Silva and G. Lochak, *Paris*
Introduction by Louis de Broglie

Earth Sciences and Astronomy

Anatomy of the Earth
André de Cayeux, *Sorbonne*

The Electrical Earth
J. Sayers, *Birmingham*

Climate and Weather
H. Flohn, *Bonn*

The Structure of the Universe
E. L. Schatzman, *Sorbonne*

Applied Science

Words and Waves
A. H. Beck, *Cambridge*

Operational Research
A. Kaufmann, *Sorbonne*